Arjun Parthasarathy is imparting to investors all the knowledge absorbed from his twenty year stint in financial markets. His website "investorsareidiots.com" is followed by investors both in India and across the globe and is acknowledged by retail and professional investors alike for its high quality analytical content.

Arjun started his writing career in 2005 by running a weekly column on fixed income markets for the newspaper *DNA Money*. His column was the first of its kind as it brought the esoteric world of fixed income to the layman and is now the most widely followed fixed income column by anyone interested in the fixed income markets in India. He is also a valued contributor on investments and financial markets to the Internet publication Firstpost.com.

Arjun's knowledge of financial markets comes from his stints in proprietary trading in banks, fund management in mutual funds, equity research in an institutional broking house and floor trading in a stock exchange. He is a postgraduate in economics and finance.

The RICH Investor

HOW TO AVOID COMMON INVESTING MISTAKES AND BUILD WEALTH

Arjun Parthasarathy

VISION BOOKS

www.visionbooksindia.com

www.visionbooksindia.com

Disclaimer

All investments are subject to risk. The author and the publisher disclaim all legal or other responsibilities for any losses which readers may suffer by investing or trading using the ideas or methods suggested in this book. Readers are advised to seek professional guidance before making any specific investments.

A Vision Books Original

First Published 2012
Reprinted 2015, 2018

ISBN 10: 81-7094-852-5
ISBN 13: 978-81-7094-852-0

Sketches by Manjul
Research Associate: Ravikanth

Published by
Vision Books Pvt. Ltd.
(Incorporating Orient Paperbacks & CARING imprints)
24 Feroze Gandhi Road, Lajpat Nagar 3
New Delhi 110024, India.
Phone: (+91-11) 2984 0821 / 22
e-mail: visionbooks@gmail.com

Printed at
Saurabh Printers
67A-68, Ecotech 1, Extn 1, Kasna, Greater Noida
Uttar Pradesh, India.

Dedication

~

This book
is dedicated to
all investors,
past, present and future.

Contents

~

Introduction

~

How Foolish Investors Make Others Rich with Their Hard-Earned Money

The cautionary theme of this book is that "Most investors make everyone else rich — but not themselves".

Think back to an investment you made which lost a lot of its value, whether in absolute terms or in relative terms.

If your investment lost in absolute terms, you lost a part of your capital forever.

On the other hand, if an investment lost in relative terms, you may or may not have lost any of your capital. But before you heave a sigh of relief, consider this: in relation to the alternate investments that could have been made, your investment has earned less — and thus you made a relative loss.

An example will provide a better understanding of absolute and relative loss.

Say an investment of ₹ 6,144 was made in a Nifty index fund on the 1st of January 2008. Nifty's closing level on that date was 6,144. On the 31st of December 2010, the closing value of Nifty

---

* I am grateful to Ravikanth for his research and help in preparing this book.

index was 6,134. The investment in a three-year period thus lost ₹ 10, assuming no brokerage costs. This is absolute loss.

On a relative basis, the investment lost 8% annually because the same money could have been invested in a three-year fixed deposit earning 8%, instead of being invested in the Nifty index fund. This is relative loss.

Now, why did the investor make an investment that lost in absolute or relative terms? If the investment was made based on a tip by a stock broker or based on a sales pitch by a salesman from a mutual fund, the investor would wonder why he listened to them at all. The stock broker made his commission by giving the tip and the salesman made his commission by selling the investment even though the investment lost money in absolute or relative terms. Thus, while the investor lost money all others have gained from the loss-making investment!

“The lesson is clear: foolish investors fund the riches of bankers, brokers, fund managers, insurers and other financial service providers. Investors themselves may or may not make money in the process.”

The fundamental of making money in financial markets is to “make money at the cost of others”. In the twenty years I spent in the Indian financial markets, there was one factor that was consistent across the investment space, and that was earning as much as you can from investors. The saying “Where are the customers’ yachts?” popularised by the book of a similar name in 1955, holds true even in this information age. The saying comes from the fact that a visitor to New York was shown the yachts belonging to investment bankers but when he asked about yachts belonging to investors, there were none. The lesson is clear: foolish investors fund the riches of bankers, brokers, fund managers, insurers and other financial service providers. Investors themselves may or may not make money in the process.

Investors come in all shapes and sizes, and most of them end up making others rich with their money. The individual investor makes a promoter rich by investing in IPOs (initial public offerings) that quickly lose value; the high net worth investor makes a fund manager rich by investing in products that generate below average or no returns; the wealthy investor makes the hedge fund manager rich by investing in funds that lose all value; and the institutional investor makes the banker rich by investing in expensive products that are prone to large capital losses.

Who is to blame for poor investment decisions that lead to others getting rich rather than the investor? In most cases, it is the investor himself. The fact is that not enough thought is given by investors when investing their hard earned money, and this is a big mistake. The whole financial services industry thrives on that mistake. The unfortunate part is that as the financial industry grows in size, fed by investors, the protection given by policy makers and regulators to the financial services industry is much greater than the protection given to investors. A prime example is the 2008 credit crisis which originated in the US. The government and the US Federal Reserve bailed out the troubled banks and insurers, including Citibank and AIG, terming them "too big to fail". The ordinary investor bore the brunt of the crisis with investment losses, job losses and loss of homes — but he was not bailed out.

“Not enough thought is given by investors when investing their hard earned money. The whole financial services industry thrives on that mistake.”

Investors cannot change the nature of the markets. They can however, profit by changing the way they look at investments. This book is about common sense investing. It points out the common mistakes made by investors and suggests ways to rectify them. The book is divided into eleven chapters with each chapter highlighting a common investment theme and then suggesting ways to rectify the attendant mistakes. Each chapter is accompanied by a cartoon that visually depicts the theme of the chapter. The first chapter shows where investment losses arise and how you can avoid such losses in future. The second chapter exhorts the investor to stop and think before investing as this can save a whole lot of future heartburn. The third chapter describes why timing is important in investments while the fourth chapter puts paid to the notion that equities can only go up, up and up. Investors must not follow others blindly even if they are highly successful is the theme of the fifth chapter and why investors must keep their eyes open for right investment decisions is what the sixth chapter is about. Chapter 7 will help investors avoid investments that would not benefit even their future generations while Chapter 8 cautions investors to keep away from imitating investment activities of large investors. Simplicity in investing is the mantra of Chapter 9 and how flavour-of-the-day investments can become duds of the future is the theme of Chapter 10. Chapter 11 describes the different types of investors and takes you through direct and indirect investing.

Hopefully, by the end of the book you would have learnt how to make investments work for you and not for others. As an investor, you are the least protected of the lot while those who benefit from your mistakes are protected by policy makers and regulators, as was seen in the case of the US. Take care of yourself first.

1

~

Most Investors are Idiots

Every unsuccessful investment by an investor profits somebody else. The one who is profiting could be a company promoter or a financial product manufacturer, such as a mutual fund. It may be a product distributor, such as a mutual fund agent or an insurance agent. It could very well be a stock broker. The successful entities could include other service providers as well, such as fund rating agencies and credit rating agencies. The common thread among all these entities is that they profit even when an investor loses money. That is what I mean when I say that most investors are idiots; they make others rich with their hard earned savings even when they themselves become poorer in the process.

Are you among the growing tribe of investors who have made others rich through your poor investment decisions? Your responses to the following questions will establish the answer.

Do you . . .

1. Have investments in stocks that have lost money for you despite being multibaggers in the past?
2. Hold mutual fund products that have actually made losses for you while stock markets have given good returns?
3. Hold high cost insurance products that are proving to be expensive to maintain?
4. Have investments in companies that have lost money in currency derivatives?
5. Hold investments in portfolio management service schemes that have collapsed?
6. Hold worthless investments that were sold to you by financial product distributors?

7. Hold shares, recommended by your stock broker, that have turned worthless?
8. Hold junk-rated corporate bonds that were once rated investment grade?
9. Hold mutual fund schemes that have earned abysmal returns despite being rated highly by mutual fund trackers?

If your answer to any, or several, of the above questions is yes, then you can easily guess who profits from your investments. They are:

1. The promoter of the company whose stock you hold.
2. The asset management company whose mutual fund schemes you have invested in.
3. The insurance company whose policies you have bought.
4. The bank salesman who sold your company derivative products.
5. The portfolio manager to whom you entrusted your money.
6. The salesman who sold you loss-making products.
7. The stock broker who recommended that you buy non-performing stocks.
8. The credit rating agencies that failed to rate the bond correctly.
9. The fund tracker that did not do its homework properly.

You can, of course, shrug off responsibility by blaming others. But the others you blame are the very same people who became rich at your expense.

You can claim lack of knowledge regarding the build-up of the sub prime mortgage crisis that caused deep losses to equity markets world-wide and hence caused deep losses to your equity portfolio. You can choose to believe the company that lost money by taking positions in exotic currency derivatives claiming the losses to be a hedge gone wrong. You can absolve yourself of the expensive insurance product that you bought by claiming that the salesman promised great returns coupled with insurance cover. You can blame rating agencies and fund trackers for incompetence. You can claim that distributors defrauded you and you can rant at your stock broker for giving wrong advice.

But, finally, who made the money and who has lost money? Who is the idiot?

Stop Being an Idiot and Make the Right Investment Decisions

It's time to change. If investors don't behave like idiots and learn how to get rich with their savings, then there will be fewer other entities getting rich on their savings. Get smart and make your money work for you instead of it working for others. Investment is common sense — and profitable investment decisions are usually those which are based on plain common sense. If you look back at all the wrong decisions you made, you will find in hindsight that had you paused and asked yourself the right questions, you may not have made those loss-making investments.

Every investor needs to ask the following common sense questions before making an investment:

1. What is the intention of the promoter / management of the company whose stock I am planning to buy?
2. Why am I giving my money to others to manage?
3. Do I understand what I am buying?
4. Is there an alternative?

Check the Intentions of the Company Promoter/ Management

In the peak of bull runs you will find your friends, acquaintances, colleagues and relatives boasting about how much money they have made by investing in the stock market. They will pinpoint a few stocks where they have made a killing. For example, stocks such as Suzlon and Punj Lloyd were indeed multibaggers during the stock market rise in the mid-2000s. These companies operated in the infrastructure sector and grew very fast by increasing their debt to leverage on a growing economy. But had you bought into these stocks at their peak, by 2010 your portfolio would have lost 80% to 90%.

The intention of promoters and managements should be to increase your wealth along with theirs. The market initially embraces stocks where there is good growth potential but when it finds that a company has overextended itself in misplaced

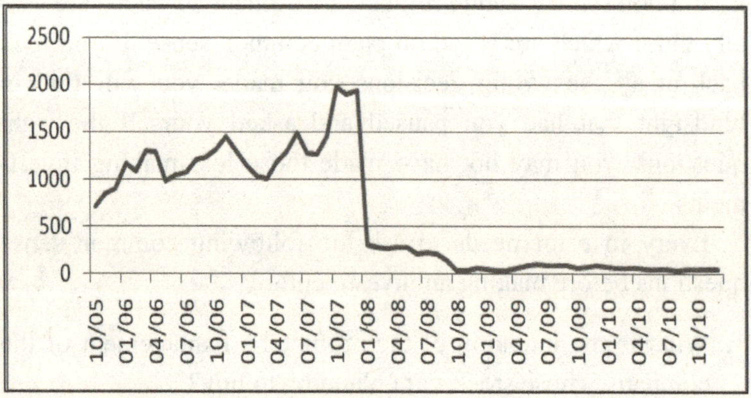

Source: BSE/NSE

Chart 1.1: **Price chart of Suzlon**

optimism, the market will drop it like a ton of bricks. That's what happened to Suzlon, a high-flying wind power company. The promoter became carried away with his spectacular rise and forgot about the interests of his shareholders. As far as he was concerned, it was unfortunate if you happened to be one of the shareholders who suffered.

There are many promoters whose only intention is to rig prices so that they can offload their holdings to unsuspecting investors. Thus, when there was the infrastructure buzz in the 2000s, or the tech buzz in the late 1990s, or the steel and textile buzz in the early 1990s, many IPOs from these sectors were floated by first- or second-generation entrepreneurs. Many of these companies do not even exist now and the stocks are duds in numerous investor portfolios. I personally hold a stock of a textile company which I bought, based on the promoter's reputation as a well-connected person. Alas, he proved to be connected in all the wrong places. The stock is practically worthless now, wiping out 99% of my investment in it. The promoter, on the other hand, is thriving and he still drives a Mercedes!

The telecom spectrum corruption scam unearthed in 2010 wiped out most of the values of the firms involved in the scam. Investors in companies such as Reliance Communication and DB Realty saw their investment values erode by over 80% in quick time. The telecom scam unearthed an alleged nexus between the then telecom minister and business houses that saw the ministry allocating spectrum to a few firms at low prices. The promoters of these firms then sold stakes in their companies to other firms at substantial gains. At the time of writing this book, these companies were being investigated for paying bribes to the telecom minister.

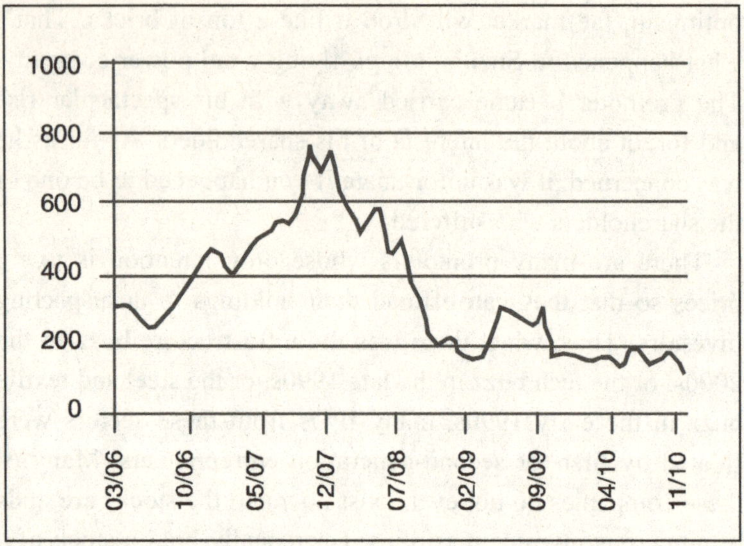

Source: BSE/NSE

Chart 1.2: **Price chart of Reliance Communications**

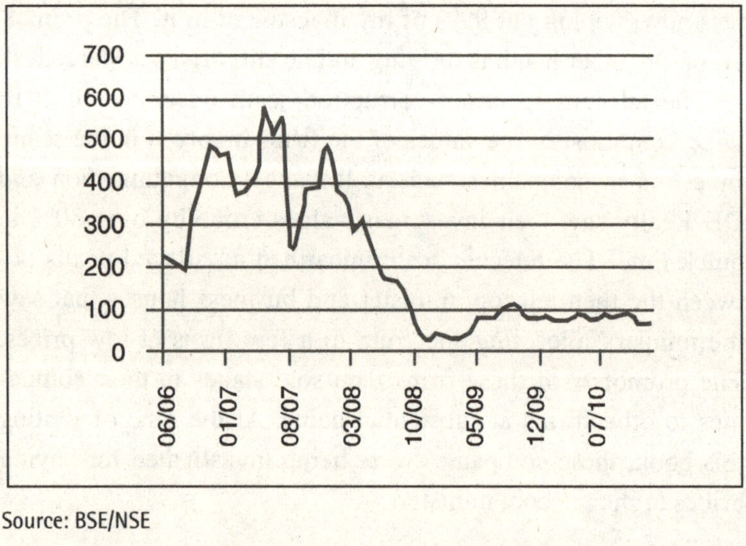

Source: BSE/NSE

Chart 1.3: **Price chart of Unitech**

Identifying managements with integrity and good intentions is tricky. Conservative managements are not necessarily good managements as they can severely trail more aggressive managements in their businesses. Equally, aggressive managements may become too aggressive and destroy shareholders wealth when business cycles turn. How, then, do you spot good managements?

One factor that never fails to separate good and bad managements is the management's dependence on financial markets. You must always ask yourself the following question:

What will happen to this company if equity markets collapse tomorrow or if interest rates shoot up?

If a company is highly dependent on the performance of the equity market or on interest rates remaining low, then it's time to relook at your investment in that firm. If, on the other hand, the performance of the company is not affected by equity markets falling or rising, or interest rates going down or up, then such firms are worth looking at for investment. Obviously, you must also focus on their business prospects when making investments even in the best managed firms.

Invest in Money Managers Who Work for You, Not for Themselves

The reason you give money to professional money managers is that you believe they will do a better job than you can in managing your money. Once you have selected a mutual fund or a portfolio management scheme (PMS), you have reposed faith in the money manager by letting him manage your hard-earned money. The money manager will have to justify your faith by managing your money to the best of his abilities. Unfortunately, a large number of money managers are more concerned about taking on your money to manage than in actually managing it properly. This is because the additional funds garnered will increase their revenues as they charge management fees based on the amount of money they manage and your money will increase the worth of the asset management company (AMC) concerned.

As an investor, you must identify the right money manager if you want to generate wealth through your investments. Identifying the right money manager, however, is not enough. You must also identify the right scheme or fund to invest in. There are many advisors who will give you advice on how to select the right fund or scheme. This advice may not be in your interest as such advisors are paid commissions to sell funds or schemes to investors — their interest lies in selling you a scheme rather than in figuring out whether the scheme is the best one for you.

As an investor you must learn to evaluate the future potential of a fund or scheme rather than just look at its past performance or listen to strong sales pitches.

Most funds / schemes are sold on past performance. Past performance is definitely not the best indicator of the future. Bull markets usually throw up very strong performances, especially by the very aggressive money managers. Returns from such funds usually fall equally sharply when markets turn against them. The best example here is a fund managed by a large industrial house which had a star fund manager. The fund manager was extremely bullish on technology stocks at the height of the technology bubble in the late 1990s. The fund was aggressively positioned in technology stocks even at bubble valuations. When the technology bubble burst, the fund returns turned extremely negative. At that time, this fund was on the recommended list of every distributor as its past performance was spectacular due to the build-up of the technology bubble.

There have been many such instances where markets threw up star fund managers who rode a bull wave to glory but left investors in the lurch when markets went against them. The fund managers and AMCs made their money — but investors lost out.

Portfolio management schemes run by AMCs and stock brokers have also seen their ups and downs. The bull run in the mid-2000s saw a large number of portfolio managers offering hedge fund-style management with concentrated portfolios of mid- and small-cap stocks. The market crash after the credit crisis in 2008 saw these schemes unable to sell their holdings and investors were forced to accept stocks instead of cash at prices which were way below the purchase price. Moreover, many of the stocks were illiquid. Many such schemes closed down leaving investors with deep losses.

Entrusting your money to someone else to manage it can go very wrong if you are not careful. The most important thing is not to get carried away by past returns and market sentiments. The rest of the job is then easy; select the most committed and the most reasonable money managers in terms of expenses and your money will be well taken care of.

> **“Entrusting your money to someone else to manage can go very wrong if you are not careful.”**

What is the commitment you need to look for? In a nutshell, fund managers who stick to a well established investment philosophy at all times. The most talked about example is Warren Buffett who avoided technology stocks even at the height of the technology boom. In doing so, he suffered huge underperformance for long periods of time. Technology stocks, however, did not fit into his investment philosophy and hence he avoided them. The subsequent burst in the technology bubble took Buffett back to where he belonged — to the top. Investors who have an idea of a fund manager's investment philosophy can even time their investments in such funds. For example, if technology stocks promise to be the best performers in the near future, it is best to invest with a fund manager who completely believes in technology and has stuck to his philosophy at all times.

Know What You are Buying

When investing in mutual funds or portfolio management schemes, or when buying investment based insurance products, do you know exactly what you are investing in or are your investments based on recommendations by salesmen? When a stock broker recommends a stock, do you ask intelligent questions other than the standard, "Will it make money?" Of course, the stock broker will say it will make money, else he is not fit to be a stock broker. Do you question derivative positions held by the company in whose stock you have invested?

If you do not know the nitty-gritty of your investments, you are ripe for being ripped off by others.

Every financial product has a cost and the cost escalates as the product gets more complicated. For example, among mutual funds an index fund has much lower cost than a mid-cap fund. A sectoral or thematic fund has much higher costs in terms of fees as well as risk, compared to a mid-cap fund. A small-cap stock carries higher impact cost in buying and selling than does a mid-cap or a large-cap stock fund. A term insurance is far more cost effective and far easier to understand than a unit-linked product. A plain vanilla forward currency contract is much cheaper than an exotic cross currency swap. Financial products using derivatives are the costliest of the lot.

"Investing in products that are cheap and easy to understand works much better than investing in products that are expensive and difficult to understand."

As an investor your aim is to maximize returns at minimum cost. You will find that investing in products that are cheap and easy to understand works much better for you than investing in products that are expensive and difficult to understand. The latter benefits the product manufacturer more than you can ever imagine.

You must know the following things about every company whose stock you invest in;

- its business,
- the reputation of its management,
- the amount of debt the company is carrying on its books, and
- the sentiment factor.

The business factor will tell you if the company is in the right sector at the right time, the management's reputation will tell about its intention, the amount of debt will tell you if the company is under, right or over leveraged for growth, and the sentiment will tell you about the company's market valuations.

The sentiment part is the most critical as well as the most difficult to understand and all "gurus" will tell you to buy when the sentiment is bad and sell when the sentiment is good. This advice is not always right as you may end up buying, or selling, too soon and thus end up with poor returns. You must always judge sentiment by your own innermost concerns, "Whether the price looks too high or not". Almost invariably you will be right. It's like buying vegetables in a market; you may or may not like the price but your decision will be based on whether you want it or not. You will not mind paying a higher price if you believe you will get satisfaction from it. The decision to pay a higher price is based on your satisfaction levels as well as affordability. Similar is the case with a stock. You have money to invest, your outlook for your own future is good and markets are in an uptrend with good sentiment. You will pay a higher price for the stock based on your own assessment of the environment and you will find that you have made the right decision down the line.

The TINA Fallacy: There are Always Alternatives

TINA (there is no alternative) is a common phrase among financial market participants. This is used at all times in bullish markets, be it for bonds, commodities, stocks, real estate, currencies, and so on. At the peak of the bond rally in India in the early 2000s, for example, bonds were seen as the only way out for investors since the economy was in doldrums, inflation was low and the market had seen huge returns from a structural decline in yields — benchmark bond yields came off by almost 7% from double digit levels over a period of three to four years. The alternative at that time was,

> **"There are always alternatives, and you must look for them even if everyone tells you there are none."**

of course, stocks, commodities and property as these were at their lowest levels seen in many years. Not surprisingly, the bond market rally subsequently fizzled out while stock, commodity and real estate prices shot up. "There is no alternative to stocks, commodities and property in inflationary times" was the constant refrain when markets were at their peaks in late 2007 or early 2008. The credit crisis caused a huge crash in these markets while bonds saw a huge rally on risk reversal!

The lesson here is that there are always alternatives, and you must look for them even if everyone tells you there are none. If you do not find investment alternatives, then look to spend. There may be times when every investment alternative is causing you anxiety. For example, if inflation is high, returns on fixed income may not compensate for inflation, stocks look highly speculative, property prices are unaffordable, gold prices are too high. At such times you may want to buy what you were saving up for, or go on a long-postponed holiday. Inflation will cause prices to go up in the economy but not necessarily prices of stocks, property and commodities. Prolonged inflation causes political unrest and leads to weakening market sentiments. A big mistake investors make is to invest just because they do not want to spend. There are investors who have made terrible investments only because they did not want their spouses to spend their money! Investing is not done just for the sake of investing. Investing should be done with an objective for generating returns that will help you in the future. Make this your bottom line for all investments you make in the future.

Once you apply common sense to your investments, you will find that your money will start working for you, instead of working for others.

~

2

~

Start Thinking for Yourself and Make Your Money Work for You

If you give the same amount of thought to your investments as you give to selecting a school for your child or buying a vehicle for yourself, your investments will work for you. Every investment has an opportunity cost attached to it. Investors often do not realize the cost, which is substantial.

Take, for example, investments in bank deposits or guaranteed returns from fixed income products. The returns need to be weighed against inflation and if they do not beat inflation, you are much better off spending the money or looking at other alternatives. A stock broker will give you a tip, which is usually a mid- or a small-cap stock. Investing based on a broker's tip will invariably mean losses as the broker will not follow up once the transaction is completed and he has earned his commission. You will be left holding the stock not knowing what to do with it; how long to hold it, and when to take profits, or cut losses. An investment in a stock recommended by a broker must be weighed against investing in a well known, well written-about large-cap stock. At least there are enough news flows on large-cap stocks for you to take better informed decisions. You will almost invariably find that returns from large-cap stocks are higher than those from investing in mid- or small-cap stocks based on tips.

What makes you listen to the broker? Usually, brokers are only as qualified as investors, if not less so. The broker exists because of the stock market and his income comes from earning commission when you buy or sell a stock. Naturally, therefore, most brokers advise you to buy or sell some stock or the other — and the advice is usually short term in nature. Brokers make money from turnover and the shorter term the investment, the better for them. This does not mean that all brokers are bad. Many of them are extremely good but their sound advice will benefit only a few as most investors would not listen to them. The reason you do not listen to good advice is because such advice involves some work and a lot of patience; work in the sense of detailing out the reason for an investment, and patience for the investment to fructify. I say this from personal experience.

Soon after finishing college in early 1990s, I started working as a floor trader in Madras Stock Exchange, a regional stock exchange that lost relevance after the advent of NSE. The markets were then on fire and since I was in the thick of the action on the trading floor in the open outcry system, the firm's clients thought I knew everything. In fact, I knew absolutely nothing, from reading a balance sheet to calculation of EPS (earnings per share). Yet I would give investors advice on which stocks to buy and sell and they listened to me as they believed I was an informed participant in the market! All these clients were successful in their respective professions, older and more qualified than I, yet they listened to me. Now, who is the idiot? Unfortunately, this still happens even after twenty years of volatility in the markets.

The same goes for investors who listen to a salesman from a mutual fund, an insurance company, or a bank. The easiest exams to pass today are the certification exams for selling financial products. Any graduate can pass these exams as is evident from the quality of financial product sales people you see on the street. Now, why would you want to listen to these lesser qualified people? You have strived hard to earn and save, and entrusting your hard earned money based on a sales pitch from low quality salesmen is idiotic. Think!

However, if you have invested in the wrong stock or financial product based on some sales pitch, you can take some (false) solace from the fact that even many top notch CFOs (chief financial officers) make the same mistake. This happens routinely where bankers sell products, especially derivative products, to corporate treasurers. The treasurer is usually extremely egoistic as he is called upon by a gamut of salesmen and offered luxury gifts, exotic travel destinations for so-called conferences, fine dining, etc. Obviously, nothing here is free and the corporate treasurer is playing with shareholder funds. One successful sale of an exotic derivative product to the corporate treasurer means that the salesman's bonus for the year is certain. The derivative will almost invariably cause a loss to its company and, in turn, to its shareholders, but it's a win-win for the treasurer as he's benefited from all the ego massage he receives. The big losses suffered by corporates in 2008 due to currency volatility were largely due to corporate treasurers playing irresponsibly with shareholders' money for their personal benefit. Again, not all the corporate treasurers or CFOs are bad but unfortunately there are not very many good ones either.

"The most irrational behaviour is entrusting your investments to relatives or friends."

Why do you behave irrationally when it comes to investments? It's your hard earned money and you should take good care of it. A wrong investment means that you have lost the opportunity to invest the money elsewhere or spend it on some of your needs. The most irrational behaviour is entrusting your investments to relatives or friends. Retired fathers or fathers-in-law are the most common money managers. They read newspapers, speak to brokers, *et al.* and dabble in stocks, property, etc. They are invariably ill-informed, tend to get swayed by market forces and usually lose money. Trusting them to manage your money is a highly risky decision. People have lost their life savings by letting their relatives or friends handle their investments.

Insurance is the worst of the lot. Insurance salesmen are usually your relatives or friends. Any graduate can become an insurance salesman, and claim that he or she is registered with the regulator. Insurance salesmen will sell you the product that fetches them the highest commissions, not the policy you need. Why, for example, would you want to take an expensive insurance policy on your child? The money is better spent in taking a higher insurance cover on yourself as your family benefits from that. With insurance on a child, nobody benefits except the salesman and the insurance company.

Insurance bundled with investments is another big investment mistake. You do not know who is managing your money and what effort goes into it. The costs are heavy and insurance companies can never get the best investment talent as investment is not the main focus of their business. You would be much better off with a simple term insurance cover and investing in a good stock or in a good fund manager.

When it comes to investing, you have to fend for yourself. No one can save you, including regulators. No one will sympathise with you either if you make a bad investment decision. Irrational and idiotic decision-making will only help others get rich, not you. Think smart and think for yourself. Then you can make your money work for you.

Thinking about Your Investments

A house can afford to have some unwanted junk lying about but not an investment portfolio. The junk in the house occupies space but at the time it was acquired it may have given you some pleasure. An unwanted investment will not give you pleasure when you acquire it and it also occupies space in your portfolio. An unwanted investment blocks your hard earned money from earning returns from better alternative investments and also prevents you from spending the money wisely.

Think many times before making an investment. There must be a solid reason for investing and the reason is not just to save. Often, Investors find some money lying in their bank account and think they must put this money away for the future. The thought process is right but you must think it through further. Saving is one thing, earning returns is quite another. Savings can actually cost you money, whether through inflation or as a result of investing in high cost or loss-making investment products. Savings should earn returns for you to benefit from in the future.

"Saving is one thing, earning returns is quite another."

Okay, so you have money and you want to save. There are so many channels available for you to deploy your money. There are also any number of people waiting to take away your money. It's easy to get carried away — or confused — by the sheer number of choices available. This is where you need to stop and think the hardest. The first idea that may come to your mind is to invest in a long term product for your child. If you do so in the form of insurance, you have done your child a great disservice. Inflation will ensure that your child's education cannot be funded from what you earn from the insurance policy. You may think of equities. Unfortunately, it may be the peak of a market bubble in which case the investment you make even with a ten-year horizon may not generate any returns and leave you disillusioned. If need be, hold on to your money till you find the right investment. Think hard on where to invest your money.

You can also make use of the very people who want to take away your money. You can get information from them, you can ask them to do research for you, you can get them to do the basic paperwork — and you can make them compete with each other to reduce your costs. Get the stock broker to give you a list of all stocks that can potentially give you returns over the time period of your investments. Get the mutual fund salesman to tell you why mutual funds are cheaper and better alternative than insurance. Get the financial planner to compare costs of every product available in the market. Find out the cheapest and the best alternatives.

Think and invest. It will save you from thinking about your investments after the investment is made and has turned sour.

I Think, therefore I Invest

"I think, therefore I invest" is the right way to look at investments. The original adage by Descartes, "I think therefore I am" suggests that an individual exists because he can think. Similarly, an investment should be carefully thought through. Once there is careful thought behind an investment, it is easy to maintain it — or take corrective action if the investment starts turning sour. Look at your current or prospective investments and think about answers to the following:

1. Why have I made this investment or why am I going to make this investment?
2. What do I do with it now that I have invested?

"Why Have I Made This Investment?"

Why is my money in fixed deposits of banks? Why is it in this particular stock? Why have I invested in this mutual fund scheme? Why did I buy this insurance product? These are all questions you should ask yourself about your investments. Once you have asked these questions, find the answers. If the answers look like the ones below, you need to relook at your investments:

- My money is in fixed deposits because I have not thought about any other investment avenues.
- I invested in this stock because my stock broker told me to do so.
- I invested in this mutual fund scheme because I was told by my financial advisor that it's a good investment.
- I bought the insurance product because the salesman was pestering me to buy it.

On the other hand, if you have thought through your investments, your answers would look like the following:

- My money is in fixed deposits because I think the time is not right to look at other avenues.

- I bought this stock because I like the company's business prospects.
- I invested in this mutual fund product because it gives me exposure to a good portfolio of stocks which is picked by a good fund manager.
- I invested in the insurance product for taking a risk cover on myself to take care of my family themselves if something were to happen to me.

"What Do I Do With it Now (or Later)?"

- "I have this fixed deposit but it's earning anaemic returns and does not even compensate me for the rise in living costs".

  Alternative options available are fixed income products floated by mutual funds which may give better returns with similar safety factors in terms of credit risk, fixed deposits of well-run companies (I do not say "highly rated" as rating agencies have proved to be inefficient in times of turbulence as was seen during the credit crisis of 2008) that offer better returns, and government run savings schemes. There are options to diversify into equities or real estate if the time looks right. Spending is always an option.
- "I bought this stock based on the recommendation of my stock broker but it's giving negative returns."

  Options are to hold on to it if the company's prospects look bright or sell it and buy some other stock if the current prospects for the company look bad. Alternate options are to move into fixed income if the stock market looks pricey. Option to hold on and do nothing about it is not a good one.

- "I invested in this mutual fund scheme and the returns are very poor."
  Evaluate the scheme and its costs. Evaluate the fund manager. Evaluate alternative schemes of the same fund. Evaluate other mutual funds. Then choose the best alternative.
- "I bought this insurance product but the premiums are killing me."
  Find the cost of cancelling the policy. Look for alternatives in terms of cheaper and easier to maintain policies. See if the future cost of maintaining your policy is dependent on stock or fixed income markets and judge the outlook for these markets. Letting the policy lapse should be the last alternative. It is the most expensive option of the lot as you have already paid out the costs of the policy up front.

~

3
~
Timing is Extremely Important

The constant refrain from anyone whose business is based on markets, especially equity markets, is, "Don't try to time the markets. Equities will give you good returns in the long run" even if you have lost your shirt and pants and have no way of investing more money into the markets. The reason for this advice is past data; stock indices have moved up since the time they were formed.

This advice is not true in all cases. For example, you may not have been born when the markets were showing an uptrend or may not have had money to invest in the markets at such times. It is even more unfortunate when you finally have some money to invest and find that you have invested at market peaks or bubbles, and you have actually lost capital over long periods of time. Your inopportune investments would have killed your appetite for investing in stocks so that when the time is right to invest, you will baulk at doing so.

Markets have their boom-bust cycles and it is imperative to time these cycles. Most of the time, it is circumstances that make you money in the markets. Sometimes it is foresight, which is highly creditable. Timing is true in other aspects of life as well. For example, someone who played cricket for India in the 1970s will regret not having been born later. The money earning capacity of cricketers is far higher now than what it was forty years back. Someone born in the 1960s and entering the workforce in the 1980s was definitely not as successful as a person born in the 1970s and entering the workforce in the 1990s. The tech boom and the opening up of the economy created many job opportunities and that

"Markets have their boom-bust cycles and it is imperative to time these cycles."

generation of workers have done well for themselves. However, someone born in the 1990s and entering the work force around 2010-2011 would have found the going much tougher given the extreme competitiveness in businesses.

The same goes for investing. Indian investors have benefited most by investing in equities in the first decade of the 2000s. Three-year returns for the Sensex (Bombay Stock Exchange Index) were in the range of 25% to 40% CAGR (compounded annual growth rate) while five-year returns were in the range of 20% to 40% CAGR. Investors who invested in the Sensex in the early or mid-1990s saw returns coming in at low single digits — or even turn negative for three- and five-year periods. Ten-year returns from the Sensex have been the best for investors who invested in the late 1990s rather than the early 1990s. Ten-year CAGR returns ranged from 3% to 20% if one had invested in the Sensex in the 1990-2000 period.

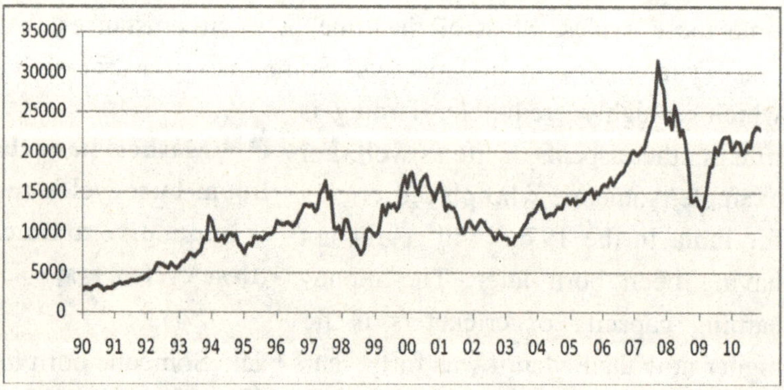

Source: BSE

Chart 3.1: **BSE Sensex, 1990-2010**

A similar story was played out in other markets as well. Investors investing in the US and European markets (Dow, Nasdaq or FTSE, for example) saw the best returns in the 1990s while the first decade of the 2000s saw returns plummeting, or even turning negative. Japan has been the worst of the lot with consistently poor to negative returns over most part of the last two decades. Hong Kong and other parts of Asia saw two sets of returns; one in the early 1990s leading up to the Asian crisis in the late 1990s, when returns were extremely good in the range of 30% to 45%; and the other at the beginning of the first decade of the 21st century where returns averaged from 20% to 40%. The other periods have been dismal with even deep negative returns.

Some of us are lucky enough to have been in the markets at the right time and at the right place. An investor in India investing in the late 1990s was much better off than investors

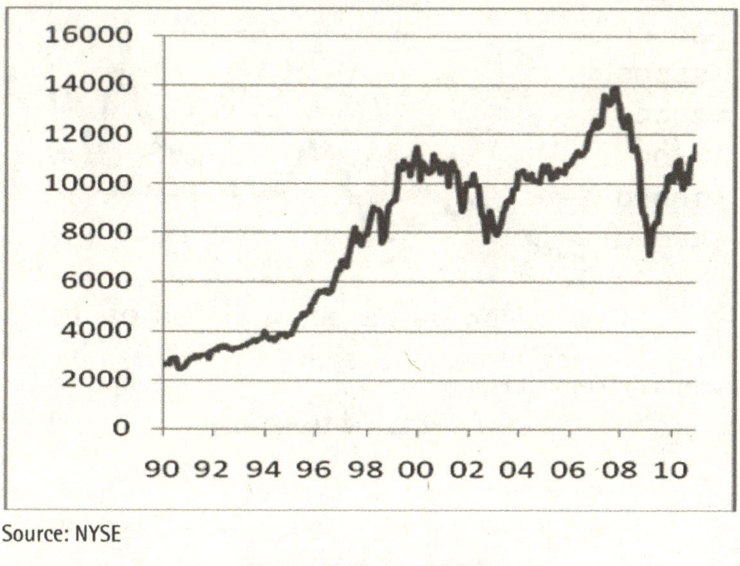

Source: NYSE

Chart 3.2: **Chart of DJIA**

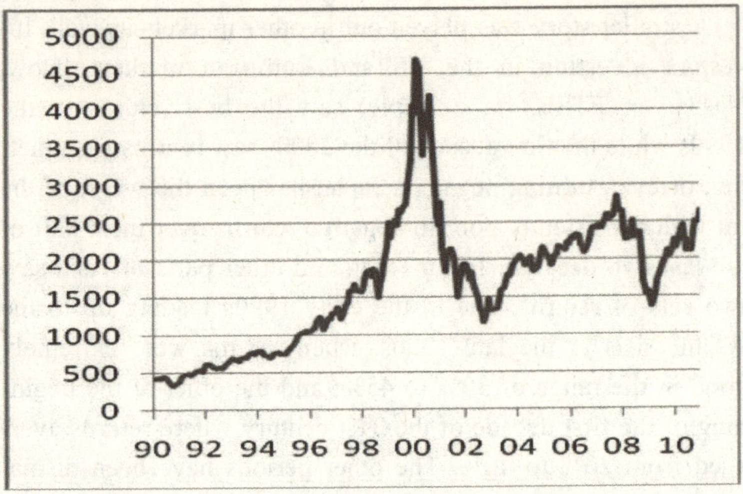

Source: Nasdaq

Chart 3.3: **Chart of Nasdaq Composite Index**

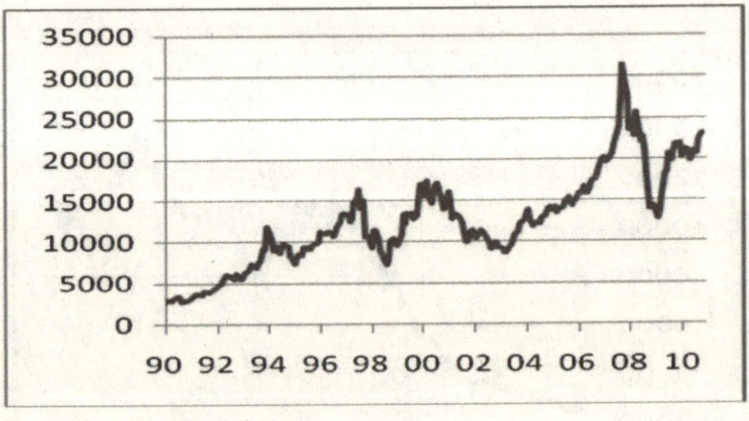

Source: Hong Kong Stock Exchange

Chart 3.4: **Chart of Hang Seng**

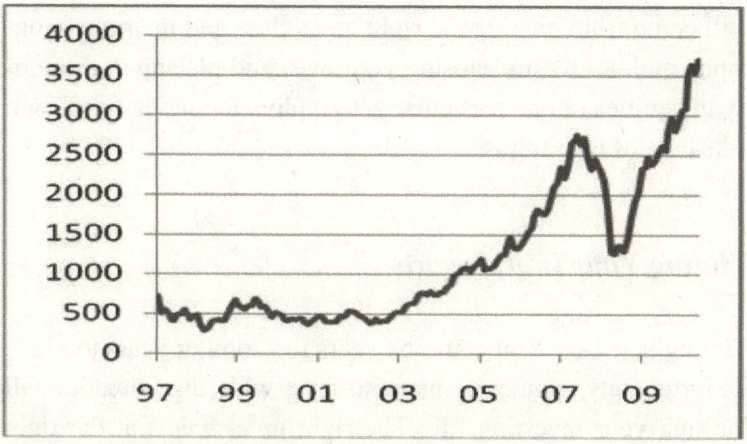

Source: Jakarta Stock Exchange

Chart 3.5: **Chart of Jakarta Composite**

investing in, say, Hong Kong or Korea at the peak of the Asian bubble in the late 1990s. It was, of course, pure chance if you were born an Indian and had investible surplus then. It was lucky timing. However, having investible surplus in India may not be the best situation to be at the time of this writing and you would have been better off being born elsewhere where the market outlook is much better!

As an investor, you have no choice but to live in the present. The past is gone and what exists is only the present. In the world of finance, the present is an outlook of the future and as an investor you would have to determine whether the present is discounting the future correctly. If the future is being over-discounted, it is time to sell or avoid investing — and *vice versa*. Unfortunately, you do not have a time machine where you can place yourself at the most opportune time for investing. You will have to evaluate the choices available to you and pick the one that suits your line of thinking. Irrespective of asset class or geography, what is certain is that your returns will come from picking the right asset class and the right geography and not by just closing your eyes and placing your money in equities of one particular geography, hoping that time will take care of the returns.

Timing Your Investments

Timing is tricky. You could be years too soon or years too late. Unfortunately, you will have to live with this situation all through your investing life. The right investments at the right time can protect you from multiple mistakes later on. However, wrong investments at the wrong time can prevent you from ever investing again. The words of Warren Buffett ring true many times: "Buy when everyone one else is fearful, sell when everyone else is greedy."

However, you will find that often when everyone else is fearful you do not have money to invest and only when everyone else is greedy do you have money to invest. How do you then time the markets?

Introspection is one of the best ways to time the market. Introspect on whether the market makes sense to you and if you do not get the right answers then avoid investing till you get the right answers. Now, this raises the issue as to how to answer the question "Does the market make sense to me?"

Let me give you the example of my own stint on the trading floor of the Madras Stock Exchange. The markets were red hot when I started. That period is now known as the "Harshad Mehta time". Stocks were on a singular move upwards, and yours truly enjoyed the rise. I did not know anything about investing in stocks then; I was fresh out of college and had not even learnt how to calculate basic ratios. The system was not as well developed as it is now and was fraught with risks, right from settlement risk to counterparty risk. There was a complete lack of awareness of these risks at all levels and investors and speculators alike ignored all risks as they were making lots of money since the market was on a one-way up trend.

I was sure of one thing then. It was not due to my great expertise that I was seeing returns in the market but due to the market itself. It did not make sense to me and I was sure that something was wrong somewhere. I quit the market and went on a long holiday with the money I had earned. Then the securities scam of the 1990s broke out and the markets crashed. Many of my friends who were high-fliers in the market at that time went bankrupt and many of them have completely stayed out of the market ever since. Careers were ruined and lives broken. I will be the first to admit that I did not have a clue about any scams. I was simply extremely lucky to have gone out at the right time. However, the fact that I did a bit of introspection and went out to get some answers helped me avoid a disaster early in my career.

“ Timing is always clear in hindsight ”

Timing is always clear in hindsight. In real life, one can never time markets to perfection but with a little bit of introspection, and a little bit of luck, one can be reasonably good in buying and selling at the right time.

So, what is it that you should reflect on when looking to buy and sell stocks?

Professional investors will tell you to study various economic, financial and market data, including levels of interest rates, levels of inflation, corporate profitability, volatility indices, etc. All this is far too difficult and beyond the scope of a typical individual investor. Also, all these data tell you what happened in the past and not what's going to happen in the future. Professionals will then tell you to look at forecasts given by economists and analysts. Forecasts are just forecasts, however; they will always go wrong. The bubbles and busts of the past were predicted by only a few and those few, too, could only predict one or two of the numerous bubbles and busts.

You are the best timer of the market for your investments. In times of market uptrend, you will notice things happening around you. Friends and relatives who had not got job offers for some time will land themselves good jobs. Your own prospects in your organization or business will be improving and you will be more confident of your cash flows in the future. If you own a house, its price will increase in value or you will have been able to buy a house for yourself given your own job prospects. You will find yourself thinking of saving and where to invest your savings. This will generally be the right time to invest in the market.

"You are the best timer of the market for your investments."

On the other hand, you need to start worrying when you find that the actual business environment is not as good as the markets make it out to be. You will be working harder to make the same amount of money or even less; your organization may have built up leverage and is now struggling to service interest costs; you will not be able to afford a house as prices will have gone up significantly; or the value of your own property and stocks would have gone up so high that your children / friends who have recently started their working career may not be able to buy what you could at the same age. This is the time to sell.

You will not always, most probably never, be able to buy at the very bottom of a trough, nor sell at the very top of a peak. You should aim to act reasonably close to peaks and troughs, and while this can cost you a lag of a year or two, it will be well worth it, as you still have an investing career ahead of you.

"You will never be able to buy at the very bottom of a trough, nor sell at the very top of a peak. You should aim to act reasonably close to peaks and troughs."

The best example of timing was given to me by one of my friends. He was greatly solicited by wealth managers and advisors at Sensex peaks of 20,000 in the late 2007 and early 2008. He received calls every minute, asking him to invest in one or the other stock or financial product. Then the credit crisis bubble burst and the Sensex fell to 8,000. After that there was not a single phone call from the very same people who had sold him stocks and products aggressively at market peaks. Now they did not even whisper a recommendation to buy at troughs. Moral of the story: the best time to sell is when everyone is hounding you to invest while the best time to buy is when everyone is pressing you to sell.

Your own life is an example of the importance of timing. If you are in the right place at the right time, you are lucky. Let's take the example of working professionals who are just starting off their careers or have been working for a few years. In the earlier part of the 2000-10 decade, such professionals could buy a house in a metro city for around two times, or less, their gross annual salary. Inflation then was in the low single digits levels. In 2011, similar professionals would have had to fork out four to five times their gross annual salary to buy an equivalent house as inflation climbed close to double digit levels. Who is luckier in terms of timing?

The worst possible time is when you come into money at market peaks. You are afraid to invest, yet you have money and past returns have been very good. You then plunge into the market only to find that the bubble has burst. An investor I know made this mistake in early 2008 when the Sensex peaked out at 21,000. He came into some money, got carried away by the prevalent hype about energy, infrastructure and power sectors and invested in new fund offers from mutual funds. The fund NAVs are still below par even after three years, despite Sensex regaining most of its losses.

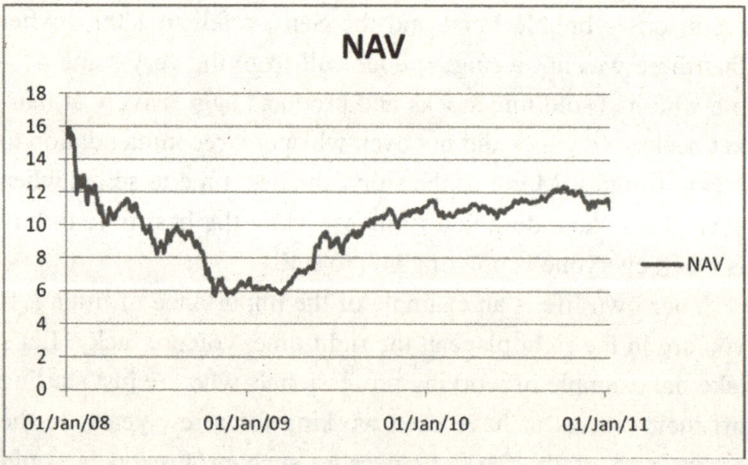

Source: Reuters

Chart 3.6: **NAV of UTI Energy Fund Growth**

Natural disasters, acts of terror, political upheaval and other such unforeseen events lead to large volatility in the markets. You will find your portfolio losing value overnight and gains of many years get wiped out in the matter of a few days. You cannot obviously time the market to wait for such events, but you can keep taking profits periodically from your portfolio and reinvest those profits when such events occur. Profit taking is a healthy activity, even though you may rue it if values continue to go up. At worst, you would have lost out on opportunity of further gain — but such opportunities will always come back time and again.

~

4

~

Equity is Not a One-Way Street

The constant mantra dinned into the heads of investors by everyone — from stock brokers to a politicians — is that equity markets will always go up and will always give good returns. Stock brokers promote equity investing since they earn brokerage commission when investors buy or sell shares, while politicians recommend investing in equity since good equity markets help create a feel-good political climate. But the stock broker forgets you once he has earned his brokerage commission while politicians come and go. The investor, however, remains invested often only to lose money. Other market participants offer similar advice. Mutual funds will always peddle equity as they earn bigger management fees on equity assets. Insurance companies selling unit-linked policies will always ask you to invest in equities as they can then sell policies which are more lucrative for them. Business channels, magazines, newspapers, research publications, newsletters, technical analysts, authors of investment books, economists, policy makers, stock tipsters, financial planners, etc. all recommend equities as it suits their business. Investors fund them by following their advice.

"Remain invested in equities for long periods of time and you will make money" is the easiest advice to give, especially when markets have done well in the past. This advice is particularly enticing when markets are at record levels but at times when markets have fallen sharply from peaks, this advice appears to be meaningless. Long term market returns may look good at times of market peaks, but will look awful if considered over a period encompassing falling or stagnating equity markets.

The advice about not timing the market comes at bubbles when most individual investors actually enter the market looking at the handsome returns of the recent past. Later, when the bubble bursts, the investors are left with stocks bought at the highest prices and are forced to hold them for long periods of time if they don't want to sell at a loss. Investors who buy at the wrong time may not see returns for over a decade. In that period, typically, a middle-aged industrial worker would have put his life's savings in the market and by the time he is due to retire, his savings would actually have not made any money.

Some would say this is not applicable to fast-growing economies like India and China. The markets do not bear out such optimism. A saver who invested his money into bubbles in the 1990s in India did not see returns for over ten years. By that time, he would have lost all appetite to invest in the markets. A saver who invested in the early 2000s, on the other hand, would have seen excellent returns on his investment but that is not the case for the saver who invested in the market in the late 2000s. Equity investments are, therefore, not a one-way street. Stock prices will go both up and down.

The markets will always exist and anyone having money to save will have to look at the markets for investment. Often when the stock markets are at peaks, other things may also be at a high — property prices, job prospects, bonuses, etc. — but when the bubble bursts, everything comes down with it. A bonus received when the markets are at their peaks is best kept away in a safe rather than being reinvested in the markets. This is typical of companies, too. Booming markets tend to give companies unjustifiable expectations of the future thereby encouraging them to take unreasonable risks with their assets instead of preserving cash flows. A market collapse brings down even well-run companies who have been carried away by market excesses.

A market collapse is very hard to digest.* Investors see their hard-earned savings disappear. Usually, the anticipated gains from equity investments are spent in advance and when actual returns are non-existent, investors are stuck with large liabilities. Lives are broken, families are split, health problems occur, etc., when such notional wealth fails to materialise. Bubbles bring about the hardest falls. One day your neighbour is the cynosure of all eyes with his perceived wealth, the next day he is a failure. In India, property and stocks have a high correlation. Stock market gains are usually invested in property and when the stock market collapses, property markets follow. The investor is left with nothing at the end of t he collapse except high debts due to leverage on real estate.

"In India, property and stocks have a high correlation – when the stock market collapses, property markets follow."

Market veterans who have seen cycles will tell you about the hard times they faced and stories of how many of their friends and colleagues could not survive a market collapse. Only a few emerge better off, and those who have a special survival instinct. As an ordinary investor who's looking to save for the future, it is always better to be a prudent equity investor than a "close your eyes and it will go up" one.

---

* Mine was a family of successful stock brokers — pillars of society, members of top clubs, close to industrialists, etc. The stock market collapse of the 1990s wiped out the wealth effect, and the success is now only memories.

Asset Allocation is the Easiest Advice to Peddle

Asset allocation is the most abused word in the investment dictionary. Anyone in the investment world who has nothing to say but wants to sell something, will advise asset allocation. Asset allocation means investing in different types of assets, such as bonds, equities, commodities, real estate, currencies, etc., giving different weights to each asset class. It is easy to advise investors to allocate their savings in various asset classes. The premise is that by doing so investors benefit through diversification. Equally, it is an excellent device for an investment advisor or a financial salesperson to cover his ineptitude.

Why should an investor pay these guys who advise asset allocation? Asset allocation does not require any brains. Take an Excel sheet, give weights to each asset class, plug in an expected outcome, and voila!, you get the expected returns. A more "professional" advisor will take into account your age, career progression, etc. to allocate assets. As per the asset allocation model, equities will never fall in the long run, bonds will always give back your money, and gold, property, commodities, etc. will always keep rising. How else does one explain investing in all these asset classes at one go? If the belief is that equities will always keep rising, commodity prices will always go up, property prices will always go up, why then invest in all of them? Take the best asset class of the lot (in terms of liquidity, expected returns, etc.) and invest only in that. Equities will always come out on top and one may as well be invested fully in equities rather than allocate one's money to different asset classes.

No advisor or financial product peddler worth his salt will leave out equities as an asset class. It is the easiest thing to recommend, especially in bull runs, and the time horizon will always be three to five years. Now, just think what happened to investors who followed this advice in US, Europe, Asia, Japan, etc. where equity markets have not given returns for a decade. Returns would have been good if one had invested at bottoms and sold at tops, but then that is a matter of timing, and no asset allocator will advise timing equity markets!

Markets Will Bounce Back

"Equity is a one-way street — it always goes up. If it ever falls, the market will bounce back. Buy on dips." How often have you heard this? Actually, each point contradicts the other. The first is that equity prices will never fall, so remain invested in the markets. The second is that while equity prices do fall, they bounce back, so hold on to your investments, or invest afresh. The third suggestion is to buy when the market falls. You must have realized by now that none of this advice works. If you had remained invested in equities at the peaks of bubbles, you will see your portfolio value disappear after the bubbles burst. "The markets will bounce back" is good advice only when the markets have lost their bottom — but you have to sit and nurse your losses till the markets recover, if ever. Remember, you were never given the advice to sell at peaks! "Buy, as the markets have bottomed out" is good advice, but where is the cash? You have

"The markets will bounce back" is good advice only when the markets have lost their bottom

invested all your money based on the fact that equity markets will never fall; now markets have fallen and you do not have the money.

Also, there is a difference between investing in equity indices and investing in individual equities. There is a tendency to speak about market indices rather than individual stocks. However, in bull runs, you will always be advised to buy individual stocks or stocks of a particular sector. When the market falls, the advice will then become "invest in the indices". If you had bought individual stocks, then you may or may not see returns even if indices bounce back. You must be careful about what you want to invest in — whether it is the index or individual stocks.

The equity market — whether it goes up or down — will always exist. The market can have long periods of uptrend, long periods of downtrend, and also stagnate for long periods. If you have been lucky in the uptrend period, then you must look to cash in on your luck. Periods of downtrend or stagnation will leave you with less money to invest, but even small investments can grow to become big investments once the markets come out of their pessimism. Equity markets are definitely not a one-way street and the sooner you realize it, the better your investments will work for you.

What are the Alternatives?

Unfortunately, there are very few alternatives to equities. The equity market is the most visible, most transparent, most regulated and the most accessible. The market is available to retail investors at the lowest cost, information is freely available and returns on equity are the most lucrative if investments are made properly. The alternatives to equity are fixed income, real estate, commodities and currencies. Of these alternatives, fixed income and real estate are the most prominent amongst investors. The other markets, i.e. commodities and currencies, are not really meant for retail investors as they are mostly traded on a derivative platform which is highly volatile in nature.

Fixed Income Investments

Strange as it may sound, the concept of fixed income investing is relatively unknown to the average Indian investor even though fixed income investments play a very large part in an investor's life. In India, a part of your salary goes into provident fund and pension fund investments that are almost fully invested in fixed income securities*. You would invariably have money parked in fixed deposits of banks or corporates. If you are a bit more knowledgeable, you will be invested in fixed income schemes of mutual funds. However, fixed income as a return-generating asset class and as an alternative to equities is not prevalent in India. Fixed income can offer equity-beating returns if timed well. One period when

> **“Fixed income can offer equity-beating returns if timed well.”**

* Funds, which have investments in equities, largely in the developed economies, have seen values erode on equity investments. One of the largest retirement funds in the world — the California Public Employees Retirement System (CalPERS) — faced huge depreciation in its assets in the market crash of 2008. There are various estimates to the size of the losses but the bottom line is that the retirement funds' assets do not balance with the obligation to its members.

fixed income investments outperformed equities in India was during 1999-2003 when there was a secular decline in interest rates, while equity markets were suffering from weak sentiments. Returns on investments in government bonds and corporate bonds (directly or through mutual funds) averaged over 15% in that period while returns on the Sensex averaged a negative 11%. There was also a brief period in 2008 when fixed income returns were over 20% while Sensex returns were a negative 50%.

Individual investors are primarily invested in fixed return schemes, such as provident funds and fixed deposits. Some retail investors may have investments in post office savings schemes, National Savings Certificates and other such government sponsored schemes. The intent of the government in promoting such schemes is to channelize savings into productive assets, especially infrastructure assets. However, the government typically uses this money to spend on social schemes and subsidies — and as the government collects more under these savings schemes, the higher the interest costs they have to pay. The government then uses collections under these schemes to service debt which leads to a Ponzi-like cycle. The returns under these schemes are fixed and are usually below the inflation rate as the government uses the monies collected under these schemes unproductively. The investor is actually incurring real negative returns by investing in such schemes, especially when inflation is running high in the economy. A simple back-of-the-envelope calculation will show you whether such fixed income investments are generating sufficient returns to beat inflation. Work out your own cost of living index (do not believe official statistics) by calculating the expenses that dominate your life. If these expenses are rising much faster than the returns earned by your fixed income investments, you are generating real negative returns on your investments.

How do you time fixed income investments? The basic principle is that price of a tradable fixed income instrument (bond) is inversely related to the yield (level of interest rates). If interest rates fall, prices of fixed income instruments go up while if interest rates go up, prices of fixed income instruments go down. If prices go up, then investors get capital gains and if prices go down, investors lose capital. The best time to invest in fixed income investments in order to generate better returns is when interest rates are expected to go down. You can invest in fixed income schemes run by mutual funds or buy government or corporate bonds to benefit from a fall in interest rates.

"The best time to invest in fixed income investments is when interest rates are expected to go down."

Real Estate Investments

Owning a house typically takes up all your savings in your initial saving phase. Once you have bought your first home and your cash flows stabilize, you then look at other investment avenues, such as equity. Many investors, however, do not look at investments other than property. The reason is that they have seen property values appreciate sharply — and in case they have borrowed to buy real estate, their sense of profits is much higher. However, buying property for your personal use and real estate investing are quite different. Real estate for investment must be looked at in relation to equity investments.

Usually, equity investments perform better and with more transparency and liquidity than real estate investments. Borrowing to invest in real estate as an investment exposes you to the risk of fluctuation in real estate prices. If prices drop, then you are left paying EMIs (equated monthly instalments) on a losing investment.

Real estate investment is similar to equity investments in some respects. Past returns determine your decisions while builders and brokers are out to take your money away from you. Often, you end up owning property you never really wanted, and if you don't invest at the right time, the property burns a hole in your pocket. You tend to borrow and invest, and servicing the interest eats into your ability to diversify into other asset classes. Many a time, you cannot sell your property as either there are no buyers or the prices quoted are too low for you to sell. Builders delay constructions when their own fund flows dries up and that affects your liquidity.

"Real estate investments made to upgrade your own living standards will benefit you the most. Else, it benefits builders and brokers while you are left servicing interest costs."

Real estate investments when made to upgrade your own living standards, will benefit you the most. Else, it benefits builders and brokers while you are left servicing interest costs. Unlike equities, owning real estate involves many costs. There are property taxes and maintenance charges to be paid. You are susceptible to changes in laws. Your tenant may give you trouble. If you own land, it may be encroached upon. Your builder may have by-passed taking some clearances and your property may not be completed on time. You must think many times before investing in real estate as a form of investment.

There are real estate funds that give you access to real estate without the headaches and costs associated with owning a property. These funds are like mutual funds and act as collective investment schemes that invest in real estate. This is a better way to invest in real estate than buying property. However, these funds come at high costs, are illiquid and susceptible to property busts. Timing is important when investing in such funds.

Here is a typical example of an associate of mine who got carried away by real estate. He approached me for advice on his investments. I studied his existing investments. His portfolio consisted of 1% stocks, 5% ULIPs and 94% real estate. His money was going in servicing the interest on property loans and in paying ULIP premiums. His real estate investments were under-performing while ULIPs were out-of-the-money by a long margin. He knew he had to rid himself of some real estate investments but the impact cost of selling property was very high as brokers quoted him prices much lower than the perceived market prices. Do not let this happen to you.

~

5

~

Don't Listen to Market Pundits

Numerous people claim to be stock market "pundits". Each pundit will have some claim to fame — either he is managing money in an institutional capacity, or he has made money in a bull run. These pundits constantly offer investment advice. However, their advice is generic and vague, and no advice will be forthcoming when things start going wrong. If you invest based on their advice, you will almost invariably lose money, especially if the markets are volatile. These pundits also constantly talk about their investment positions and how well they expect their investments to do, but when things turn against them, they vanish from the horizon.

You will never find a fund manager telling you to sell — or not to invest — at peaks; peaks are the bubbles and troughs are the bottoms when the bubbles burst. Fund managers will always tell you not to time the market. That is because they earn their fees by the size of assets under their management. Any market participant earning fees or commissions from the market will always tell you to stay invested even if you are losing heavily and there is no possibility of recovering your capital in the near future. It is foolhardy to act on their advice. Most of these pundits would have made money only in bull markets. Long periods of market stagnation or downtrend will reveal their true colours.

"Any market participant earning fees or commissions from the market will always tell you to stay invested even if you are losing heavily. It is foolhardy to act on their advice."

These pundits offer bad advice, to say the least. But what is unfortunate is that people actually act on their advice quite mindlessly, which results in a grievous loss of money. The best advice you can get is — use your own mind. After all, it's your money. Not all advice is bad but usually good advice is ignored since it does not fulfil one's greed. Smart people make money by capitalizing on other people's greed. Investors are considered to be idiots who can satisfy one's greed thereby making them the most sought after people in the world.

"Smart people make money by capitalizing on other people's greed."

The most sensible thing to do is to use your own mind to separate good advice from the bad, and use it to make money. Trust your instincts; they will usually be right. Be willing to pay for good advice; anything which is cheap has strings attached to it.

The Worst Peddlers of Free Advice

- ***Business Television Channels:*** Business television channels cover the stock markets throughout the day. They rope in investment "pundits" and a few technical analysts and talk incessantly about stocks, indices and charts. They also get a few investment professionals to talk about the economy, policies, investments, etc. Using information received from a business channel to make investments is a certain way of losing money. There is absolutely no substance in these channels; it's all show business.
- ***Politicians, Especially Finance Ministers:*** When markets are moving south relentlessly, politicians usually advise everyone "not to panic". One can lose the shirt from one's back by staying invested based on this advice.
- ***Internet Newsletters, Web Sites:*** There are numerous Internet-based publications that offer sub-standard stock market

advice. This advice leaves one holding worthless investments with no possibility of ever recovering one's money.

- ***Newspapers and Magazines:*** These publications carry investment recommendations either by outsiders or their own staff who are typically unqualified.
- ***Friends and Colleagues:*** They will usually repeat the tips they receive or the stuff they have read. Most of the time they will not invest in the stocks in which they advise you to invest. You will end up losing your money following such well-meaning but useless advice.

A market bubble always throws up more and more free advice. The aftermath of bubbles is pretty interesting. An investor who had invested on the basis of free advice will find himself holding worthless investments with no further advice forthcoming from the same free advice givers. The same newsletter, politician, magazine, etc. would no longer offer any advice. Even if they do, all they would say is — "Hold on to your investments. Everything will be alright." The so-called "best advice" that one receives is at such times — "Markets are overheated; they will correct", "We advise profit booking at these levels"; "corrections are healthy", etc. The next line of advice is — "Buy on dips. The markets will correct; remember equities can never fail." Almost invariably, when these "pundits" forecast corrections, markets take the contrary path — they rise much further. Similarly, when they advise that it is the right time to buy with a view that markets can only rise from existing levels, markets fall even further. The same experts who tell you not to time the markets will always invariable make you time markets!

Their safest advice during times when markets move southwards is: "Average it out!" What to average — a stock that has lost everything and has no hopes for the future, or the broad index? Suddenly, the index is the topic and not individual stocks. These advisors invariably recommend individual stocks when markets are rising; they don't talk about the index. When the market is falling, the investor is left holding worthless mid-cap stocks while the advice now being rendered is to buy the index, or average out large-cap stocks.

Mutual funds offer SIPs or systematic investment plans. "Invest at all levels" is their mantra. They advise investing a small sum every month. Unfortunately, the markets would have peaked much sooner than you thought and you would, in all likelihood, be investing at peaks and, almost invariably, you will increase allocation at peaks. Then markets fall with a thud and you are back to where you started.

Market pundits are always given prominence. They are present in the electronic media, the print media, in round table discussions, in public forums, etc. They talk about markets and about investments. They are given prominence for a reason. The reason is that they say what you want to hear. "You are safe investing in equities or debt", "You are making the right investments", "You will make your required return in a few years' time", etc. In short, they are saying that you're doing the right thing by investing. They will go on to talk about the country's growth story, what policy makers are doing to make the country more efficient, how good the corporate sector is and the fantastic job the central bank is doing. They appear to be a front for politicians, which, in fact, they often are; You may as well be listening to a politician making an election speech!

> **"Market pundits are always given prominence. They say what you want to hear for a reason."**

What makes you listen to them? What makes you believe the finance minister when he insists that everything is alright, when you actually do not want to pay taxes to a government which you know is not doing the right things with your money? You know you are losing money on your investments and yet you continue to listen and act on sweet talk. Bear in mind that sweet talkers are usually after something, and in the case of financial markets, they are after your money. The quickest way that they can get rich is to make your money work for them.

How to Use Free Advice to Your Advantage

Free advice has its advantages. You can glean some useful information from free advice. You can then use this information to do your own research. This will benefit you more than investing mindlessly based on the free advice doled out to you.

In an equity market where there are more than 8,000 listed stocks, it is very difficult for an investor to study so many stocks before investing. Let the free advice givers do that for you. You can look at the universe of stocks that is discussed in the media. You can then shortlist stocks you would have an interest in, and then consider investing only in those stocks that fit your investment profile. There is a lot of analysis done on macro economic data. You can get analysis on inflation, interest rates, consumer spending, industrial growth, government finances and other such data. Based on these analyses, you can judge for yourself where the economy is heading. For example, you will always hear corporate sector heads saying that the government is doing a good job, but when you actually go and look at data analysis, you will find that the data is throwing out horrible numbers on inflation and government finances. This will put you away from investing till such time that you find improvements in these parameters.

The Internet is a treasure trove for information. In the world of Twitter, Facebook, blogs and other such networking or opinion sites, you can always find any information you want. If you are interested in a particular stock or if your broker has recommended a stock, you can seek information on the stock through these sites. There will always be someone somewhere who can give you a correct picture on the stock. There could be a disgruntled customer of the product or a disgruntled client. There could be an investor who's had a bad experience with the stock. You can get information on the quality of a company's management. You can get information on financials from someone who's done an in-depth analysis of the company's account statements. There is no end to the information you get once you start searching for it. Use this to enhance your investment capabilities.

"It is worth paying for good independent analysis if you are serious about investing."

The Internet allows you to access research reports by market professional including stock brokers, economists, independent research analysts and others. These research reports are highly informative and more or less give you the real picture of a company. Institutional investors will look at all angles when investing in a stock, and research reports cater to such investors. You can arrive at a fair judgement of the company if you read these reports. Read and obtain information from these reports but refrain from mindlessly accepting the advice given in them. Analysts are usually more prone to giving "buy" recommendations as that earns them brokerage. Independent analysts are better and have no bias, but their reports are not always free. It is worth paying for good independent analysis if you are serious about investing.

6

~

Don't Ignore What You See Right in Front of Your Eyes

Often one has certain warning signs right "under one's nose", so to speak, which one tends to overlook either because of following the herd or sheer indifference. Two such obvious signs are bubbles and depressions.

Investors fail to recognize bubbles in spite of the situation staring them "in the face". During bubbles, asset prices are at such inflated levels that cash flows do not justify the prices. One would have to stretch one's imagination to figure out where the returns will come from. Almost all bubbles, at peaks, will price shares of companies at the profit expected at least five years in the future. What these figure simply is that the bubble will continue to grow forever! Similarly, property bubbles are there for everyone to see, but guess who gets caught — you! When property prices are driven by liquidity and not supported by real cash flows of property buyers, then there is a bubble. When property bubbles burst, they take years to correct. In the meanwhile, EMIs have to be paid on property values that may have halved. Property developers, who have taken money from you, will default on loans to banks. Typically, large developers will have political and criminal connections and would have stashed away their ill-gotten wealth while defaulting on loans. However, when you default on your loan, banks will come down heavily on you. In spite of bubbles appearing so often in the past and teaching investors a lesson, when the next one appears, investors make the same mistakes and get caught in the bubble thereby suffering financial losses.

"Investors fail to recognize bubbles despite of the situation staring them "in the face".

Similar is the case with depressions. In spite of values of stocks and properties being at extreme lows, you may see your own prospects looking bright as companies' cash flows stabilize, businesses get restructured, and employment prospects brighten. However, sentiments in the markets will continue to remain dim due to market excesses taking a beating. This is a time when your own ability to save increases as the inflation rate will typically be low. This is the time to put your money in stocks. But investors usually refrain from investing during these times due to the low market returns of the immediate past; they do not want to risk their capital. To benefit from a depression, be observant. If you find that business activity is picking up, job prospects are looking bright, and consumption is increasing, then maybe it is time to invest in equities. However, when there is excess all around, it's time to take away money from the market. Always sell when there's a buyer available and you think that the prices are right, and buy when there is a seller available to offer the stock at a price that is acceptable to you.

" Due to the herd mentality that investors suffer from, buyers will invariably vanish when prices fall and sellers will vanish when prices rise. "

Due to the herd mentality that investors suffer from, buyers will invariably vanish when prices fall and sellers will vanish when prices rise. You will almost inevitably buy or sell at around 10% to 20% above or below the lowest or highest price the stock has reached. However, this 10% to 20% will save you much more as your purchase / sale turns out to be a right decision. Do not wait for the last rupee.

The "Last Rupee"

There are countless instances of investors having lost money by waiting for the "right" price or the "right" time. No one can predict where the markets will head; you don't know where it is headed even the next minute. If you have arrived at the "right" price or the "right" time in the past, it was perhaps due to sheer luck and not necessarily foresight or knowledge. You need to look at the broader picture when taking investment decisions, and if you start micro managing the broader picture, you will always lose. This attribute is seen among all investors, including professional investors. Equity fund managers keep waiting for the "right" valuations to buy, and it will never happen; by the time they buy the stock, the price would have gone up sharply. Bond traders wait for the "right" yield to sell; that yield will never come, and they will end up losing a lot of money by selling at much higher yields. Similarly, investors wait for the "right" time to buy stocks; that time will never come and they will buy at much higher levels. Property buyers will bargain for the "right" price, and by the time they finalize a price, another buyer would have quoted a higher price and taken the property away. The original buyer will then end up buying at much higher prices — the last rupee costs a lot as seen in these cases. Unfortunately, investors always compare financial markets to vegetable markets where bargaining to the last rupee is the order of the day. In financial markets, the last rupee is the most expensive one in terms of loss that you would have ever borne.

> **"Once you have seen the broader picture, it makes sense to avoid micro-managing to the last rupee."**

Once you have seen the broader picture, it makes sense to avoid micro-managing to the last rupee. Where buying stocks is concerned, if you have done your homework and are convinced that a particular stock is a good long-term buy, then waiting for the "right" price does not really make sense unless you believe that the market is overheated. If you think the market is stable, then waiting for the "right" opportunity to buy is as good as letting good returns go. Market participants are very speedy in spotting opportunities, and while you are waiting for the "right" price, you end up losing that much more in returns as the stock price keeps moving northward. Similar is the case when selling stocks. If you believe that the stock price has reached the optimal level and you are ready to sell, waiting for the "right" price will only result in you selling at a much lower price. While you would have been right in terms of the broad picture, you would have lost while trying to micro-manage the small picture.

The Markets Don't Wait for You to Act

How many times have you regretted not doing something that you wanted to do? Markets are rife with instances of investors willing to sell or buy, but not going through with the transaction because of one reason or the other. The cost of not carrying out the transaction can be enormous. Take for example instances where potential property buyers had identified the right property to purchase, the right seller and had concluded that the price was reasonable. Yet, the transaction did not go through because the buyer was unwilling to close the deal at the exact price the seller wanted, which was a mere 5% higher than the buyer's offer price. This is clearly a case of being obstinate, which costs the buyer heavily. Another buyer enters the picture and picks up the property at the price the seller wants and closes the deal in a jiffy. By the time the original buyer identifies another property, the prices may even have doubled.

Equity investors, or even stock brokers, would have stories to recount on how they lost "good" opportunities. Common stories include, "I wanted to sell my portfolio as I was worried about the market, and I had enough gains, but by the time I got around to giving orders to my broker, the markets were down 25% and I did not have the heart to sell then." Unfortunately, this was also witnessed in the case of stock exchange cards that were available for sale during the early 1990s. At that time, stock brokers in India saw the value of their stock exchange memberships go up to astronomical levels. India had opened up its economy and stock markets were witnessing very high volumes with brokers making good money. Stock exchange membership rates went up even in case of regional stock exchanges. I know for a fact that some members of the Madras Stock Exchange, a regional stock exchange, wanted to encash on the rise in membership value and were close to striking deals with potential buyers. However, many deals did not go through because the sellers became greedy and wanted higher prices than what the buyers were quoting. Later, the National Stock Exchange (NSE) was set up and destroyed membership values in regional stock exchanges, including the Madras Stock Exchange, and members saw their worth falling by 95%. The market did not wait for the sellers to sell at the "right" price.

What is "the Obvious"?

"The obvious" implies that there is some event or situation that is impending, and although you are aware of it, you ignore it. There are two reasons for this — either you don't want to face the event or situation, or you don't want to believe that it will happen. An example of this in the movies is if citizens of a town ignore a dormant volcano spitting fire believing that it will not erupt, till it actually does. In real life, it may be a health problem which you know you have but do not do anything about till it becomes serious. In the investment world, it is the excesses you see around you, which you know are excesses but you ignore till they erupt.

The excesses you see during booms will be malls coming up in a place where there are already too many malls, your neighbours buying expensive cars which you know they cannot really afford, companies making expensive leveraged buyouts that can only be justifiable to the analyst or the investment banker who is doing the deal, your son or daughter making more money than you in the stock markets, and so on. The stock market crash of 2008 was caused by banks' excessive lending to weak borrowers in the US hoping that rising property prices would take care of the debt servicing costs. Property prices crashed, banks went bust, and markets all over the world collapsed. These times can be trying; you know there are excesses but you do not want to act on your knowledge because you may miss the "last rupee" gains. Look at the broad picture, listen to your reasoning, and act on it.

Markets are Like Fair-Weather Friends

Successful people, especially politicians, dictators and rich businessmen, are courted by many who want to extract either some favour or money out of them. The most recent examples are of the dictators in Tunisia, Egypt and Libya. These dictators made huge amounts of money at the expense of their citizens, yet they were courted by politicians from developed economies, educational institutions, businessmen, bankers, entertainers, etc. Each of these followers wanted to gain from the ill-gotten wealth of these dictators. When these countries faced a public uprising, all the so-called friends of these dictators vanished; some of them even opted out of their high positions because of the embarrassment of being associated with dictators and profiting from the association. When these people were courting the same dictators, it did not take long for them to realize that the dictators were plundering their country for their own personal benefit. Yet they chose to look the other way since they too were making money out of their association with these dictators.

The markets are similar. As long as the going is good, one never stops to question why the market is doing well. You should. As the markets go higher and higher, one becomes blind to the negatives visible in the system. For example, in the events leading up to the credit crisis of 2008, bankers noticed the unstable nature of the mortgage loans they were buying and selling, but chose to ignore it as the immediate profits were too attractive to forgo. Citigroup suffered the most due to the crisis.

> **"As long as the going is good, one never stops to question why the market is doing well. You should."**

Navi Mumbai in the Year 2000 – Real-life Example of a Property Price Bubble

Navi Mumbai, although a part of Mumbai, is a bustling city by itself. Navi Mumbai was developed as an alternative to South Mumbai. Town planners wanted to shift government offices from South Mumbai to Navi Mumbai. Unfortunately, the idea was a decade ahead of its time. The planners went ahead and built the infrastructure, which included wide roads, spacious railway stations, good residential accommodation, quality educational institutions, hospitals and commercial places. The property bust of the mid- and late 1990s affected Navi Mumbai, and property prices collapsed. Real estate was available at half the peak rates that prevailed before the bust. The economy in 2000 was just coming out of a recession though the property market was four years away from spotting it. That was the best time for entry into property in Navi Mumbai.

By 2010, property prices had soared six-fold. Navi Mumbai is now a hotbed of real estate. It is booming with malls, hotels, schools, colleges, businesses, etc., and the international airport project is slated to take off. However, property prices are at a peak and are unaffordable to most. While one could buy property at twice his income in Navi Mumbai a decade ago, in 2010 one had to fork out almost four to five times one's annual income. Inflation has hit the income earner hard, and the buyer will have to struggle to pay the monthly instalments on a loan.

The real estate price in Navi Mumbai was definitely not affordable for the real buyer in 2010, but investors continued to speculate based on the airport project. It is certain that the speculators will lose money, unless incomes of prospective property buyers double or treble in the next few years.

In the year 2000, growth prospects for Navi Mumbai were obvious; by 2010, they were murky. The excess was obvious.

The head of Citigroup at that time said, "We will dance as long as the music is playing." Citigroup shares lost almost all their value after the crisis hit and the group had to be bailed out by the US government.

It is wise to stop and think about why you are making money, especially if the gain is quick due to a surge in prices of stocks or property. If you do not find the right answers, then you must act by taking your money out, else your paper profits will vanish into thin air.

Did You See It but Still Ignored It?

Here are some examples:

1. Your company was starting to earn quality profits with margin expansions, and yet you did not invest in the stock or the stock of its competitors.
2. Head hunters had been pursuing you with better job offers, but your savings were still in fixed deposits.
3. There was construction work taking place near your residence; a number of people were visiting real estate brokers and concluding transactions, yet you did not buy property there.
4. Your friends had been buying second and third properties without having the necessary cash flows to match the cost, with the hope of selling the property at higher prices, and you too jumped on to the bandwagon without independent thinking.
5. Your friends and relatives were raving about the IPO of a prominent company; you applied for shares in the IPO

without studying its prospectus. The price of the share is half today.

6. Your own cost of living had been going up while your income levels were lagging; you knew that this meant a high inflation rate in the economy, but you were still heavily invested in stocks.
7. Prices of stocks that you knew were worthless started going up sharply, but you tried to profit from the price rise.
8. You were offered loans by banks beyond your repayment capacity, yet you invested in stocks of the same banks.
9. Your company started facing headwinds due to many factors, yet you did not encash your stock options at a profit.
10. Your friends and relatives were dabbling in stocks and talking about their success, which you knew was not due to their investment capability, and still you tried to emulate their success.

~

7
~
When One Year Becomes Three Years

The "one becomes three" phenomena underlines how an investment originally made with a one-year return horizon suddenly becomes an investment with a three-year return horizon. Typically, this happens because the investment would have collapsed in value due to a market correction. While it is not always advisable to get out of such an investment, most times it will pay to shift your money elsewhere. This decision will, of course, be based on the factors surrounding the collapse. Many investors carry investments that have no place in their portfolios but exist only because of the one-becomes-three factor. In many cases, three also becomes five — and five becomes forever. The gainer here could be a next generation inheritor but not you. It's, however, better to see returns in your lifetime than in the next.

"When an investment turns sour, the original reason for it is forgotten and convenient new reasons are found to hold on to it."

When an investment turns sour, the original reason for it is forgotten and convenient new reasons are found to hold on to it. This leads to retaining assets that never perform, or significantly under-perform, as compared to other investment categories or the broad market as a whole. By not exiting from bad investments at a loss and reinvesting the money in assets that are expected to perform well, an investor loses the opportunity to recover the losses from better investments instead of hanging on to the bad ones.

Investments do, and will, go wrong. The trick is to accept wrong decisions and exit from such investments if there are no sensible and valid reasons to hold on to them. Most of the time investments turn sour when an investor gets carried away by market sentiments and looks for quick gains. However, quick gains may — and will — lead to quick losses too, and such losses should be absorbed till the next investment opportunity arises. Investors forget that there will be other opportunities and one should be ready to grab them. Holding on to investments that have gone sour prevents you from exploiting better opportunities.

Often, investors try to average out loss-making investments by putting more money in the same investment; in other words, throwing good money after bad. "Averaging out" an investment means buying more of that investment at lower prices in order to reduce the overall cost of the investment. In this case, the investor has lost touch with the reality that the investment may never ever perform. To confirm this reality, take a look at all the dud stocks that have fallen from peaks and stayed down even in the best of bull runs. The same money could have worked much better in a winning investment.

Similarly, investing continuously in a rising market may work only for a while. As prices continue rising, you would have to evaluate the future return potential from each fresh investment. Even though you may be buying blue chips, doing so at market peaks is a mistake; they can fall very fast and may never see the same peak prices again for a very long time. Adding to stocks in a rising market without looking at the future potential is as bad as adding stocks in a falling market without looking at the future potential. In other words, keep your eye on the future potential of an investment in all situations before putting your valuable money in it.

Three Can Also Become One

The reverse of "one becomes three" is also true. In rising markets, when you make an investment with a time horizon of, say, three years, you may find that you have made substantial gains in the first year itself. In such a case, consider whether you should still hold it for the full period you had originally planned, or would it be better to book profits in the first year itself. To make the correct decision, you must again look at the future potential of the investment rather than the gains you have made in the past year. If you believe that the future potential is good and you are willing to hold it for a longer period of time even at changed valuations, then you can do so for the period of time that you are comfortable with. If you find an alternative investment that will potentially give higher returns than your current one, you can shift out of your existing investment and use the money to invest in the more promising investment.

Investments that are fundamentally sound but witness rapid rise in prices are worth holding on to — but at reduced or zero costs. In other words, if your investment has given good returns, you can sell a part of it to reduce your original investment, or even make it zero. You get to enjoy dividends or capital appreciation, or both, on your existing holdings without worrying about potential losses. For example, if you had bought 1,000 shares of Stock X at ₹ 100 per share for a total value of ₹ 100,000, and the price has doubled to ₹ 200 per share, you can sell 500 shares at ₹ 200

> **"Investments that are fundamentally sound but witness rapid rise in prices are worth holding on to — but at reduced or zero costs."**

per share where you will receive ₹ 100,000 as the sale amount. This amount is what you had invested initially, and the rest of the 500 shares of Stock X become free of cost for you. In fact, if you do this consistently across your portfolio, you will be the proud owner of a good portfolio of stocks that are free for you and earning good dividends if they are stocks of good dividend-paying companies.

You must remember that every boom is led by one or two particular sectors and, after the bust, the sectors that led the boom lag for long periods of time. The market boom in the 1990s, for example, was led by the technology sector. After the sector went bust, technology stocks lagged behind the market for eight years. After out-performing the BSE Sensex by a whopping 230% at the height of the boom in 1999, the BSE IT index under-performed the BSE Sensex by 17% CAGR in the period between 2000 and 2008. Similarly, the market boom in the 2000s was led by the infrastructure sector, and after the bust in 2008, infrastructure stocks lagged the Sensex. The BSE capital goods index lagged the BSE Sensex by 6% CAGR in the period between 2007 and 2010. The capital goods index had out-performed the BSE Sensex by 25% CAGR in the period between 2003 and 2008. You must always shift from out-performing sectors after busts, and move into the broad market till you find a sector that is likely to perform better than the broad market.

“You must always shift from out-performing sectors after busts, and move into the broad market till you find a sector that is likely to perform better than the broad market.”

Forget the Past and Focus on the Present

You can avoid holding on to investments for longer than you need to by viewing them the way proprietary traders assess their positions. Proprietary traders evaluate their positions on a daily basis and what matters to them is the current price, not the previous day's price. The only reason to hold on to positions is if the trader has a view that prices will go up from current levels. Alternatively, the trader will hold on to his positions if the prices are expected to fall from current levels if he is short in the market. If the positions don't fulfil this criterion, the trader will get out.

As an investor, you can treat your investments in the same way. Your investment value is what it is at present, not what it was yesterday or what you paid for it originally. Yesterday has come and gone, and if you have made profits, that's good; if you have made losses, well, too bad. You must judge the future performance of your investment from current prices, not at the prices at which you bought it. If you hold 500 shares of Stock X at ₹ 200 per share, you need a valid reason to hold on to the 500 shares. If you believe that the stock will give good returns from the current price of ₹ 200 per share in a specific time horizon, which could be anywhere between one month to several years or more, you have a valid reason to hold on to the stock. If you believe that the stock will not do well from current levels and is likely to come down for various reasons, you should not hold on to the investment and should sell it instead. It does not matter whether your purchase price of the stock was ₹ 100 per share or ₹ 1,000 per share. What matters is whether the stock price will go up or down from the current price of ₹ 200 per share. You need not undertake this review exercise every day, but once a year is definitely advisable, and more frequent reviews will not harm your portfolio. In very volatile markets, do an ad-hoc review of your portfolio to take quick decisions, if needed.

Getting rid of unwanted investments will help you make attractive profits from your future investments. Firstly, it frees up your money and readies you to look at fresh investment options. Secondly, it does not tie you down to your existing investments. Thirdly, it makes you consider alternatives which can potentially generate higher returns. Lastly, let your investments work in your lifetime and not for the generations to come.

> **“Getting rid of unwanted investments will help you make attractive profits from your future investments.”**

Stars Yesterday, Duds Today

Every investor who has been through market cycles would usually have some duds in his portfolio. These dud stocks are either not traded or are quoted at such low prices that it is not worth selling them and incurring transaction costs. However, these duds were once stars in the market, and that would have been the reason you bought them. Innumerable stocks become duds because of changing market conditions. The reasons could be many; promoters vanishing with the money, the business becoming too competitive, technology becoming outdated, and other such factors. It is the same for retail shops. If you look around your neighbourhood, there will be some shops which have been running successfully for long periods of time, while some shops open and shut quickly. As an investor, you will have to separate long-standing businesses from businesses which come and go. You will not want to hold duds in your portfolio. Remember that for every dud, there is also a large-cap stock that has given manifold returns. If you had gotten rid of the duds quickly by reviewing your portfolio in the manner indicated earlier in this chapter, you would have been able to buy good stocks that would have more than compensated you for your losses. Holding on to dud investments is a sheer waste of your valuable money.

Similarly, if you have a mutual fund scheme that has lost its relevance due to market factors, you are losing money every day by not shifting out of it. You pay management fees for a scheme even if it is not performing, and the blocked investment prevents you from investing elsewhere. You must quickly shift out of such schemes to avoid favouring the asset manager by giving him free money. Dud investments are charity to people who do not deserve it.

~

8

~

Never Follow Other Investors – They May Have a Different Perspective

Here is a fundamental rule — never be a follower in the investment market.

Each investor, especially an institutional investor, has a different perspective in decisions concerning buying and selling. Each investor's characteristics reflects on his money and investments; thus, following another investor without considering one's own position is a bad decision. Often, buying or selling by institutions is not based on sound logic. It is more to do with their liquidity and nature of funds. Institutions will never be aggressive sellers at market peaks. This is because fund managers prefer to stay away from selling at market highs for fear of under-performance in a rising market. Similarly, fund managers will never be buyers at market lows due to a lack of liquid funds and, again, fear of buying in a falling market. On the other hand, there are mutual funds which are not permitted to retain cash and have to be invested in the market. Obviously, they will always be buyers at all levels. Such types of funds will typically not be able to buy at market lows due to lack of liquid cash.

Then there are various types of arbitrage funds operating in the market. They tend to move indices in the short term because of the nature of their activities. They typically move in a herd, and all their positions will have a corresponding hedge. To the individual investor, this will look like informed institutional activity but actually it's based on Excel spread sheets.

Then there are "star" fund managers or investors. These "star" investors will be able to take strong tactical calls on their investments, but they have a keen eye on the risk they run on their positions. While they do not leverage on the positions, not all their investments perform and, typically, those will be the ones you would have bought thinking that the "star" investor cannot go wrong.

As an ordinary investor, you will never be able to comprehend the reasoning behind the buy and sell decisions of institutional investors. This inability to understand their investment decisions should be the prime reason for not following their actions. If markets fall, no investor is safe. And prolonged bear markets spare no one.

The market closely tracks the activities of fund managers, large investors and well-known traders. Their investment activities are reported in the media. There is a halo cast around them, which makes other investors blindly believe their investment decisions to be the wisest ones. These investors have a huge following of "herd" investors doing exactly what they do. This usually leads to a whole lot of heartburn for the "herd".

It is practically impossible for an individual to understand the thinking behind a large market player's investment decision. The successful ones will definitely have a defined level of risk in mind before making an investment. Usually, they will ignore short term losses on their investments for long term gains. These investments may also be sold due to a change in business conditions or market environment. Sometimes a fund manager may only be straddling the index when buying stocks. If you follow and mimic market activities of these players, you will invariably go wrong in your own strategy.

"It is practically impossible for an individual to underst-and the thinking behind a large market player's investment decision."

Firstly, you may not know how much money to invest when following the "star" trader, and if you are over-exposed to one investment, any short term losses will create a big hole in your pocket. Secondly, you will not know when that star trader sells the investment or why it's being sold, and you may be left holding a weakening stock. Given that such nuances will not be available to you, it is unwise to copy others, especially the famous ones.

Categories of Investors / Fund Managers

There are many categories of institutional investors and fund managers. Investors in each of these categories have different perspectives about their investments. Some are highly regulated and have to go strictly by set guidelines while some will have a unique individualistic style. There will be hedge funds that follow programmed trading strategies, while some of them may have relative trading strategies. There are mutual funds that focus on certain types of stocks while some of them may focus on particular sectors. The list is long and as an investor, you have many choices from which to decide which strategies may work best for your money. It is better to entrust your money to institutional investors than to copy their actions. Placing your money with a fund manager helps you exit from the fund if the manager fails to grow your wealth. However, if you decide to make your own investments merely by following a fund manager's actions, you will not know what to do with your investments once you have made them, especially when they go into deep losses.

"Star" Individual Investors

Investors in this category have their own investment style and philosophy. These investors are extremely successful with their investment decisions over the years, and every investor tries to emulate them. Investors who have entrusted their money to them have ridden on the success of such individuals. These individuals may either manage their own funds or manage other investors' money. The common characteristic of these individuals, apart from their success in investments, is their commitment to their investment style and philosophy. They will not waver or be shaken from their beliefs even if they witness long periods of markets riding on factors other than the fundamentals in which they believe. It is extremely difficult to emulate their style unless you have the same belief.

Such individuals are often used by market players to sell stocks / products, etc. For example, your broker may tell you that Stock X is a good buy because a "star" individual investor or fund manager is accumulating the stock. You will be tempted to buy based on the stock broker's advice; after all, the "star" investor can never go wrong! The stock broker may have been right about the "star" investor accumulating the stock, but the stock may not be suitable for you in terms of the risks and holding period. The stock broker's motive behind recommending the stock to you is to help raise the price of the stock for short term gains. The stock price may go up in the near term but once the hype is over, it's back to the fundamentals. Since you would have invested in the stock without carrying out any research, if the stock in question does not perform for years, or never performs at all, you will be saddled with a bad investment. Unless you have complete belief in the investment philosophy of the "star" investor, you will not know what to do with your investment. While other stocks will rise, the stock you hold will languish. You will be tempted to sell out of sheer frustration. You will lose faith in the "star" investor; you will curse your stock broker, you will curse the investment. You never bothered to find out why the "star" investor accumulated the stock, and the reason should have been the fundamental reason for your investment decision. Most of the times, the stock will perform only after you have sold it!

Foreign Institutional Investors (FIIs)

FIIs influence market sentiments even more than individual star investors do. In an emerging market such as India, FIIs become a dominant investor group as they bring in and take out large sums of money in a short period of time. FIIs are foreign investors that are registered with the domestic financial market's regulator (in India's case, SEBI — Securities Exchange Board of India) to invest in a country's equity and debt markets.

FIIs are made up of a wide variety of investors. They would include individual star investors investing in different geographies, pension funds looking for growth markets, sovereign funds looking to diversify their assets, mutual funds collecting money from investors keen on emerging market returns, proprietary funds that carry on programmed trading or arbitraging between cash and derivatives, or taking currency risk by investing in stocks, and investment banks that sell derivative products based on emerging market stocks to foreign investors.

Buying and selling by FIIs invoke wide interest as they can potentially drive markets up or down in the short term. Investors will often hear that a particular FII is buying a stock and their broker will recommend them to follow suit. Domestic mutual fund managers will announce in the media that FIIs are bullish on the country, and stock prices will go up. Investors who invest in stocks purchased by FIIs will usually be left holding the baby. They will not know why an FII bought a certain stock or why FIIs as a category, bought large number of stocks the previous month, but were selling even larger number of stocks during the current month. They will not understand the nature of the funds FIIs are bringing in — whether they are short term, long term, value, growth, arbitrage, etc. FIIs, as a category, make headlines with the strength of their money but once you separate the FIIs into different investor categories, they are not as influential.

Mutual Funds

As a group, mutual funds will probably be one of the single largest categories of investors in the markets. In India, mutual funds offer many different schemes encompassing equity, debt and commodities, and also offer access to global markets. Mutual funds reflect the domestic investor's sentiment in the market. Mutual funds, being collective investment schemes, collect money from domestic investors and invest it in the markets. If mutual funds receive steady inflows, they end up being net buyers in the market, while if they see steady outflows, they end up selling.

As an investor, you have the choice of directly investing in the market or going through mutual funds. Mutual funds offer different products and different styles of fund management. You will have to select the product that suits you the best, and if many people invest in the same product, that particular product will garner large sums of money which will then flow into the market. For example, if you believe that equity markets will offer good returns over the next five years, you will invest in mutual funds that offer equity-based products which are managed by good fund managers. If your view is the same as that of a large number of investors, equity funds will gather large sums of money that will go into the equity markets, which could potentially take stock prices up.

Following mutual funds is similar to following an individual star investor or FIIs. You may be tempted to buy the same stock that a mutual fund manager is buying, but you will never know the background behind the fund's purchases. If a mutual fund manager buys a stock, it could be that he's received inflows and he's allocating a part of the inflows to that particular stock. He may actually be bearish on the market, or even indifferent. If you buy the stock based on the actions of a mutual fund manager, you may actually be buying into an over-valued stock, or a stock that may, at best, perform in line with the market. The same fund manager who bought the stock today, may sell the stock tomorrow if investors withdraw money from his fund. You will then end up holding a stock that you don't know anything about.

Insurance Companies

Insurance companies invest the premiums received from their policies into the markets. Insurance company investments are highly regulated as these companies have long term liabilities, and failure on their part to meet their obligations will lead to market chaos. Insurance companies in India invest in equity and fixed income markets.

Insurance premiums do not fall into one category, and investments will depend on their premium flows. Insurance premium flows can be long term or short term in nature. Long term premium flows are for traditional risk cover products that create a long term liability for the insurance company. This premium is invested in long term investment-grade bonds and in stocks that meet the parameters set by the financial market's regulator. Insurance companies will always be net buyers as long as premium flows continue. Insurance companies also offer investment-based products in the form of ULIPs (unit linked insurance plans). These products are short term in nature as investors believe that they offer risk cover as well as returns. Insurance companies invest ULIP premiums in equity and debt. These flows can be volatile in nature depending on market sentiments, so insurance companies will turn net sellers in the market if they face redemption pressures from these plans. Following the investment actions of insurance companies will not be beneficial as you will not know the nature of their investments, that is, whether they are long term premiums being invested in the market or premiums on investment-based products. You may find insurance companies selling aggressively to meet redemption pressures if more money flows into investment-based products.

Pension Funds

Pension funds manage long term funds that are meant for payment of retirement benefits. Globally, pension funds are very large investors and are accorded premium place amongst investment managers owing to their size and the nature of funds under management. In India, the largest pension fund, which is run by the government, invests only in fixed income investments, and not in equities. Global pension funds come into India by registering as FIIs.

You will be left in a lurch if you follow investments of pension funds as these funds will have very long term mandates and, given their size, will be under strict guidelines. They will invest only in large-cap stocks that are liquid and these stocks may be long term under-performers. Given their size, their impact cost of entry and exit will be high and this may eat into investment returns. You may end up buying at higher prices and selling at lower than desired prices if you blindly follow pension fund investments.

Large Investors Can Also Be Scamsters – Another Reason Not to Follow Them

Money Matters Financial Services was a well-known financial services firm with debt syndication as its most prominent activity. In October 2010, the company raised ₹ 445 crore through a Qualified Institutional Placement (QIP). The QIP was done at a price of ₹ 625.25 and the investors included Fidelity, Morgan Stanley Mauritius, Sundaram Mutual Fund, Wellington Management and Ivy Pacific Opportunities Fund. In November 2010

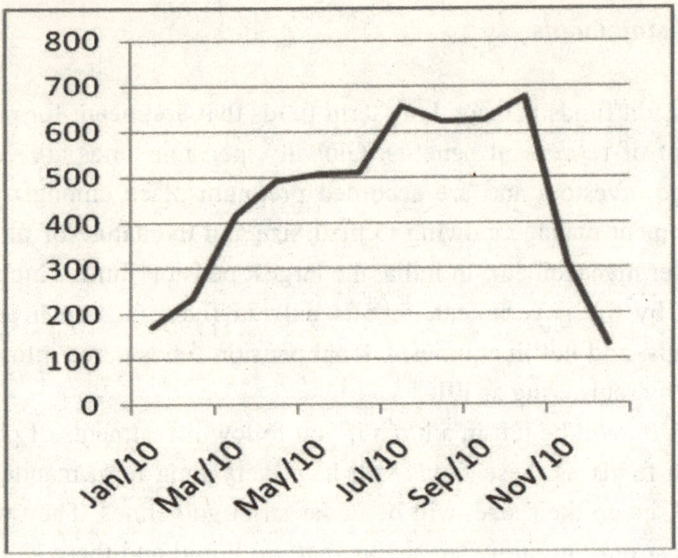

Source: BSE/NSE

Chart 8.1: **Price chart of Money Matters**

2010, the company's promoter was arrested by the CBI (Central Bureau of Investigation) on charges related to bribery. The stock price went on a downward spiral and lost more than 85% of its value in five months. Investors who bought into the stock by following the example of large investors, lost heavily in the process.

DB Realty, a real estate company, floated an IPO in February 2010, where it saw its issue fully subscribed at a price of ₹ 468 per share. The issue, with a size of around ₹ 1,500 crore, saw good institutional interest with the institutional portion being over-subscribed four times. In February 2011, the promoter of the company was arrested by the CBI for his role in

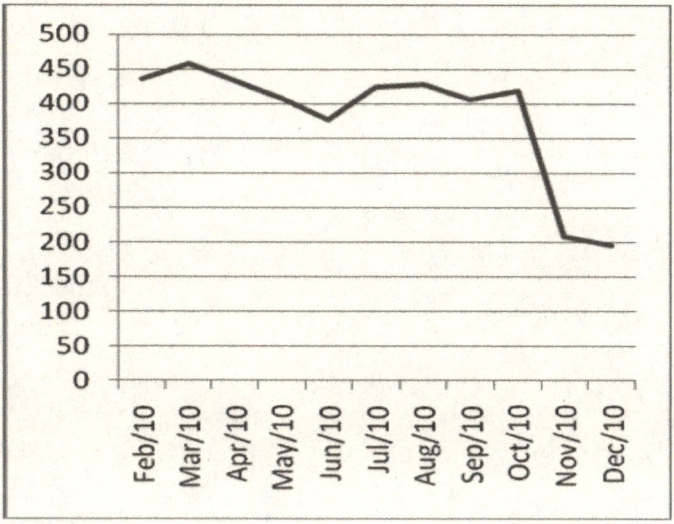

Source: BSE/NSE

Chart 8.2: **Price chart of DB Realty**

the 2G telecom spectrum allocation scam. The stock lost nearly 75% of its value from its IPO price of ₹ 468 per share, clearly proving the ineptitude of many large investors in judging promoters.

Investment bankers who were responsible for the IPO of these companies pocketed their fees but assumed no responsibility for the debacles. Investors, including large investors, let greed overcome them without doing enough due diligence and lost heavily in the process. You must never be overly impressed by "big" names, either as investors or as arrangers, and never let them influence you in your investment decisions. This includes research reports released by large brokerage houses that put out recommendations to buy or sell particular stocks.

"Investment bankers who were responsible for the IPO of these companies pocketed their fees but assumed no responsibility for the debacles."

9

~

Simplify Your Investments

Remember the popular phrase, "Keep it simple stupid", KISS in short? This is apt for your investments, too. The simpler your investments, the more money you will make. Once you start considering complex investment options to add to your portfolio, not only will your costs go up, your returns will come down as well. Complex investment options are profitable — for the seller of the investment — not for the buyer (you). Complex investments are usually illiquid. Besides, they cloud your thought process and negate the amount of homework you do for your investments. So KISS, dear investor!

Let's say that you have done a lot of thinking and research and find equities to be a good asset class to invest in for the present. Once you have made this decision, within the equity category your choices are large-cap stocks, mid-cap stocks and small-cap stocks. You will also need to figure out whether you want to invest directly in equity or use an indirect route, such as mutual funds, hedge funds or portfolio management services. This is fine because once the asset class is decided, all you need to do is to take action, that is, make your investment. Besides, this asset class offers a high level of liquidity; therefore, if things start to go wrong, you can sell in a jiffy. However, if you decide to select more than one asset class, in other words allocate your money across multiple asset classes (called asset allocation) such as equities, commodities, fixed income and currencies, you start to complicate things:

- Firstly, your cost goes up and liquidity comes down;
- Secondly, each asset class will have to be tracked separately, which will require time and appropriate knowledge to do so; and

- Thirdly, while you may be right on equities, you would have failed to generate the expected returns by diversifying into other asset classes.

This holds true for other complex investment products, too, such as capital protected products, bundling equity investments with insurance, looking at leveraged funds which use various opaque strategies, etc. Private equity and other forms of private investments also complicate your investment portfolio.

The simplification process is not applicable only to one asset class; it is also applicable to your view of the scenario in the financial markets. If you are bullish on bonds but bearish on equities, the best bet is government bonds which are a direct play on interest rates. If you are bullish on a currency pair, the best bet is direct investments, not through exotic products.

"Investment product manufacturers thrive on making investment products as complicated as possible."

Investment product manufacturers thrive on making investment products as complicated as possible. This helps them price the investment product higher and earn high commissions. These commissions are paid by investors. In other words, the more complicated an investment product, the more expensive it is for you and the more lucrative it is for investment product manufacturers and intermediaries.

Diversification is a double edged sword. If a portfolio is diversified smartly in order to capture expected returns from different securities / assets, it helps to maximize gains. Diversification done to minimize risk and reduce volatility becomes a mere Excel spreadsheet exercise. Diversification involves costs, complicates your thought process, and is not really a risk mitigation tool.

When companies can earn money through just one business, why can't an investment portfolio do the same? Often, companies that are successful in one business, diversify either to take advantage of other business opportunities, or to mitigate risk. Most of the time, this diversification strategy fails as managements do not have the necessary skills to handle the new business. This destroys shareholders' value; the money would have been better spent on strengthening the existing business or giving it back to the shareholders.

The reason for diversification should be valid and compelling. If you have invested in a fundamentally sound stock that has given you good returns, you should think many times before diversifying. If you believe that the stock has lost its ability to deliver super-normal returns, and if you have identified another stock that will potentially give you better returns, shift to the new stock completely. In other words, sell the stock you are holding and buy the new stock. If you hold two stocks, you will have to spend more time on your portfolio. Imagine the amount of time you will need to spend on your investments if you have many stocks. It's not possible to keep track of many stocks unless you are a fund manager who is supported by many analysts.

> **"If you have invested in a fundamentally sound stock that has given you good returns, you should think many times before diversifying."**

Similar is the case with mutual funds. Most funds are benchmarked to the indices and have similar portfolios. Investing in many schemes of the same nature does not make sense. Instead, it makes sense to identify a good fund manager and stick to that fund unless a situation arises that changes the nature of the fund. Tracking many funds is not an ideal way to pass time.

What is a Simple Portfolio?

A simple portfolio will reflect your investment preference. Maintaining it will not be time-consuming, and it will be easy to construct. Besides, maintaining a simple portfolio will not be expensive. However, a simple portfolio for one person may not be a simple portfolio for another as the level of understanding of the markets will vary. For example, a knowledgeable stock picker will be comfortable allocating large weights to mid- and small-cap stocks while a novice investor will be more comfortable holding well-known large-cap stocks in the portfolio. Assuming you are an investor who expects returns from equities to exceed those from fixed income investments for the next five years, your portfolio should look like the one given in Table 9.1.

Table 9.1

A Simple Portfolio

Asset class	Weight in Portfolio %	Cost of Entry / Exit	Liquidity	Overall Simplicity
Listed Equity*	70%	Low	High	Very simple
Fixed Income*	30%	Low	High	Very simple
Total	100%	Low	High	Very simple

* Direct or indirect through mutual funds.

Complications arise if the portfolio looks like the one given in Table 9.2.

Table 9.2
A Complicated Portfolio

Asset Class	Weight in Portfolio %	Cost of Construction	Liquidity	Overall Simplicity
Listed equities*	20%	Low	High	Very simple
Unlisted equities**	10%	High	Low	Not simple
Insurance linked investments	20%	High	Low	Not simple
Hybrid products***	10%	Reasonably High	Reasona-bly Low	Reasonably simple
Structured prod-ucts****	10%	High	Low	Not simple
Fixed income	30%	Low	Low	Very simple
	100%	Medium	Medium	Not very simple

* Direct or indirect through mutual funds.

** Portfolio management schemes / private equity / venture capital / hedge funds.

*** Monthly income plans, asset allocation plans.

**** Derivative products with equities as the underlying asset class.

An investor running a portfolio such as the one in Table 9.2 is exposing himself to high liquidity risk and paying high costs for 50% of the portfolio. If the returns are going to be higher than investments in listed equities, the liquidity risk and higher costs are worth it. However, when it comes to hybrids and structured products, high costs and low liquidity come with lower returns. Investing in unlisted equities is best left to professionals or investors who have a very high net worth which gives them access to the managers of unlisted equity assets.

If equity markets actually do well as per your expectations, it is obvious that the portfolio in Table 9.1 will do better than the portfolio in Table 9.2 where you are paying higher costs and suffering lower liquidity for lower returns!

Derivatives

> **"Leave derivatives to professionals."**

Derivatives are highly complex in nature though brokers will tell you otherwise since they earn excessive commissions from the derivatives market. The derivatives market has been the cause of many crises — from the 2008 credit crisis to the LTCM (Long Term Capital Management) debacle in the 1990s. LTCM was a hedge fund managed by successful bond traders and economists, including Nobel laureates. The fund devised highly complex investment strategies using derivatives and when the debt default problem by Russia hit the market, the fund collapsed and had to be bailed out by the US Federal Reserve.

You are definitely better off avoiding derivatives even if you believe you understand them very well. Derivatives are short-term products and involve realizing profit or loss on a daily basis, that is, if you incur losses on your derivative positions, you have to pay for the loss. In the case of physical assets like stocks, you just see the value go down and you do not have to pay for it. The asset you own will see prices recover in the medium to long term while your derivative positions get closed out at the expiry of the contract. You will need to spend a lot of time tracking the market as you have to mark-to-market your positions on a daily basis. You may be under the impression that you can take a larger exposure to the market by paying a small margin but once you start paying up for your losses every day, you will find that it is better to buy or sell the underlying security. Leave derivatives to professionals.

~

10

~

Beware the Flavour-of-the-Day Investments

"Flavour-of-the-day" investments are the easiest to sell to uninformed investors. That's why you must beware of them. Let's consider the example of a flavour-of-the-day stock. The stock would have given good returns in the past, it would be discussed extensively in the media, and all that you hear about the stock would be positive. However, a stock doesn't become the flavour-of-the-day very quickly. It will usually start off as a new investment theme. The first set of investors will earn the maximum returns in a short period of time. When these returns are brought into the limelight, the theme will catch up with the investment community at large. Then it gets hyped, money flows in, and a bubble starts building. Such a stock must be avoided diligently at this time; if you have invested in this stock earlier, sell right away. Don't wait for higher returns; it's too risky. The pain of being invested in the bubble is much higher than missing out the fag end of the returns at the peak of the bubble.

> **"The flavour-of-the-day buzz will swamp you."**

How does one figure out whether the stock still has returns to offer or whether it is now a bubble? The important thing is to judge whether the stock's growth potential is realistic or whether it's simply all talk by "interested" investors. Will growth exceed expectations in the next few quarters or in the next couple of years? If the answer is yes, then there is still steam left. If the answer is yes but subject to current conditions remaining the same over the next five years, then a bubble is being built. At peaks of bubbles, one has to work really hard to justify future earnings projections.

The flavour-of-the-day buzz will swamp you. The investment will be available across all platforms and will be pushed hard by every investment advisor or product manufacturer. IPOs, product launches, promoters changing their company's name, etc., are all indicators of bubbles building up. You will need a lot of will power to avoid these investments, or sell existing investments, but the gains of exiting are far higher than holding on till the bubble bursts.

A flavour-of-the-day investment will usually be owned by a large number of investors. You will find your own portfolio carrying a large portion of this investment and that in itself should be an indicator for worry. Every investment institution will have a large portion of this investment in its portfolio. At higher valuations and prices, the potential gains will reduce with the sheer weight of ownership and supply.

Technology and infrastructure sector stocks, respectively, were the flavour-of-the-day in the last two bull and bear cycles in India. Technology stocks gained prominence in the late 1990s as a result of a boom in the usage of the Internet and a rise in outsourcing. The U.S. technology index, Nasdaq, climbed to the 4,500 levels in early 2000s from around 750 in 1995. This was a whopping rise of 500% in five years. The technology bubble burst at the start of the 2000 decade, and the Nasdaq fell to around 1,500, losing 66% of its value. Even in January 2011, the Nasdaq was only at around 2,700, which was just about 40% from the highs of 4,500 seen a decade ago! India had its part of the technology bubble with many software services and product companies seeing their share prices rise very sharply, only to fall equally

> **“A flavour-of-the-day investment will usually be owned by a large number of investors.”**

fast once the bubble burst in 2000. Many prominent companies went bust and their stocks never recovered. Mutual funds jumped on to the bandwagon of technology stocks by launching technology funds. These funds were launched at the height of the technology bubble and investors were enticed into investing in these funds based on the good performance of the technology sector. Being at the peak of the bull run, the performance of technology stocks was obviously good. Once the funds were launched and collected good money, the technology bubble burst and the funds languished. Investors, who had been goaded into investing in these technology funds, lost heavily. Being flavour-of-the-day investors, they did not cash out at the right time and were left nursing their losses for long periods of time.

The infrastructure sector gained in prominence in early and mid-2000s largely due to the spectacular rise in infrastructure demand in China. The Chinese economy grew in double digits over a large part of the 2000-10 decade as an export-led manufacturing boom saw China creating huge infrastructural capabilities. The benchmark Chinese stock market index, the Shanghai Composite index, surged five-fold from around 1,000 in 2005 to around 5,000 in 2007. The market crash due to the global credit crisis, which originated in the US in late 2007, took the Shanghai Composite index all the way back to around 2,000 — a loss of 60% from its peak. In January 2011, the index stood at about 2,700, around 46% of its peak. India also had its share of market booms between 2000 and early 2008. The Sensex rose from around 3,000 in 2002 to about 20,000 in 2007, clocking a gain of more than 550%. Infrastructure stocks led the boom with stocks in the power, energy, real estate, construction, and commodity sectors generating exceptional returns, even higher than the 550% returns given by the Sensex. Infrastructure was clearly the flavour-of-the-day with many high profile IPOs from both infrastructure companies and mutual funds. The most prominent IPO was that of Reliance Power in January 2008. The company raised ₹ 11,500 crore at a price of ₹ 450 per share. There was a great amount of hype about the IPO. CRISIL, the country's premier rating agency, awarded it a rating of 4, just one notch below the top rating of 5. The issue was oversubscribed 72 times. The IPO was a flavour-of-the-day kind with the hype being the power sector, which was a thrust sector for the government. Profit projections for the company were five to seven years down the line, yet there was a huge demand for the issue. At the time of writing, the stock price was languishing at around ₹ 150 per share, a loss of 65% from the issue price.

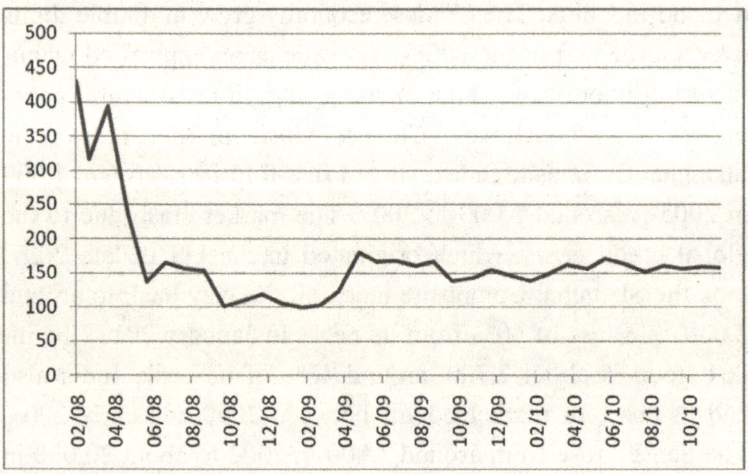

Source: BSE/NSE

Chart 10.1: **Price chart of Reliance Power**

Invest Early into the Next Flavour-of-the-Day

The right time to invest in a flavour-of-the-day stock is before the stock actually becomes the flavour-of-the-day. Investing early into technology or infrastructure stocks, and selling them at close to peaks, would have generated handsome returns. The question is — what do you look for in trying to identify the next flavour-of-the-day stock? This question is easier asked than answered. However, attempts must be made to answer the question as accurately as possible since it has the potential to generate above-average returns.

A flavour-of-the-day investment originates when it catches the investing public's fancy. From gaming consoles to fashion, flavour-of-the-day sells. Businesses that make flavour-of-the-day products make handsome profits on one product or concept alone. Recent examples of flavour-of-the-day products or services were Apple iPhones, iPods and iPads, and Facebook. These products and services caught the fancy of the public and this got reflected in their stock prices which out-performed the market by a very wide margin. Early investors in the stock of Apple (listed) and Facebook (not listed) saw their investment values go up many fold. There is no saying whether iPhones, iPods and iPads will continue to sell or if people will continue to use Facebook, but what is important is that these became flavour-of-the-day stocks.

"There is no saying whether iPhones, iPods and iPads will continue to sell or if people will continue to use Facebook, but what is important is that these became flavour-of-the-day stocks."

Look for a business or a product that is catching on fast. See if the business or product touches your daily life. It could be a service you use or a product that your children must have. It could be a product that makes other older versions outdated. It will start being used widely and everyone will start talking about it. That is the time to invest. Get out when everyone wants the investment no matter what the price, even though the price is not justifiable.

Good Times Bring Out the Worst

In the financial markets, when the "going is good", excesses get built up. Good times always end up with busts as money flows unchecked into high-performing investments. Leverage gets built into the system in search of higher returns. This is the time when one should stay away from excesses; one should avoid giving money where it should not be given. Prudence in good times will always stand you in good stead in the future. In bad times, when money should actually be put where it deserves to be invested, investors will stay away from doing so. Remember, — money invested in bad times will fetch good returns; money invested in good times will lose value.

During good times, others will attempt to profit from your savings. Suspect promoters will float suspect companies; mutual funds and insurance companies will aggressively sell flavour-of-the-day products; investment banks will sell hedged products where only they will profit the most, and novice investors will lap them up with a feeling of achievement. Good times go bad, and bad times go worse, and the "feel good" factor will vanish. Novice investors are saddled with high cost, illiquid and worthless investments weighing down their portfolios. When they should be buying, they will be ruminating about all their bad decisions.

Look at Past Returns Only if They Are Bad

Commendable returns in the past are the easiest to sell. However, being lured into investing based on past returns is foolhardy; it is usually a precursor of the markets moving the other way. Instead, you must look more closely at past returns that are poor, and see if things have changed so that returns can improve. A broker recommending a stock based on its good past returns, with an expectation of similar returns in the future, is common. It is easy to believe this; it is still easier to lose money based on this belief. Here is a pertinent question — how many brokers tell you that a stock has not done well in the past due to certain valid reasons, but conditions have now changed and the stock is likely to do better in the future? Look for this kind of advice — it will help you make profits. Here is an example of such a situation. In 2008, as equity markets were falling, bond markets were doing well and bond investments were giving good returns. The bond market was emerging from a four-year bear run. However, investors failed to capture the bond rally which was recognized by investors only at its fag end. They invested based on past returns and lost money. In other words, they looked at good past returns and went by it. Instead, they should have looked at the past bad returns offered by the equity markets and invested there because equities rose when the bond markets started moving southward.

11

~

Types of Investors

If you believe that all investors are the same, think again. Investors differ from one another based on their mindset, attitudes towards their investments and their risk-taking ability. Investors can be categorized from the "know-it-all" investor to the "know nothing" investor.

The common thread amongst most investors is an irrational behaviour towards their investments. The know-it-all investor will have money invested in the dumbest of products. Investors who have made lots of money will still invest in products that will never again generate decent returns. Investors who have never made money will still follow advice from investment quacks. Investors who have lost money on their investments will stop investing altogether, or will never learn from their mistakes. The best investor is the one who focuses on his investment strategy; he is the smartest investor.

1. ***The Know-it-All Investor:*** This investor would have made money in bull markets and will preach investments to you. He will rubbish advice from investment professionals and will invest in worthless investment products. Investment product peddlers will be able to use his ego to sell him worthless investment products.
2. ***The Dumb Investor:*** This investor is usually a successful professional. He will claim to have no knowledge of investments. He will foray into the markets on the urging of others and will usually invest modest sums. He will never learn to make money by investing right.
3. ***The Punter:*** He will largely take bets on equities and, sometimes, on commodities and currencies. The punter usually follows questionable technicals and fundamentals

and will follow incomplete or suspect information. He usually goes wrong with his investments.

4. ***The Martyr:*** He will lose money by investing at the peaks of bubbles — and will then complain about being cheated. He will start forums and write to the press and regulators to have his voice heard. His investments usually result in losses.
5. ***The High Net Worth Individual (HNI):*** He is courted by a large number of investment product peddlers; this helps nurture his ego. He makes more money for the investment product peddlers and intermediaries than for himself. He will give his concurrence to invest in products by merely casting a casual glance at incomprehendible Excel sheets, and end up paying huge costs.
6. ***The Amateur Investor:*** Housewives and students fall in this category. Usually, they foray into the markets only during bull runs. They may profits initially but then become overconfident and lose money. When the market starts moving southward, they will divest completely with their tail between their legs.
7. ***The Once Bitten Twice Shy Investor:*** This kind of investor would have lost a significant amount of money in the markets in the past; he will now be extra cautious before re-entering the markets. As a result, he will lose good investment opportunities. In spite of being so cautious, he will again lose money when he re-enters the market.
8. ***The Buy High and Sell Low Investor:*** This investor will wait for a market correction to invest; however, impatience will get the better of him and he will then invest at peaks. When the market tanks, he will become extremely nervous and will sell hastily; then he will again wait for corrections.

9. ***The Indifferent Investor:*** This category includes top notch professionals in the fields of arts and science. They fall in the high income bracket but have no interest in investments. Wealth managers have a field day with them since they don't focus on earning from their investments. They simply feel good that their money is invested and is not languishing in their bank savings account.
10. ***The Smart Investor:*** This investor is the best of the lot. He has a clear focus on returns from his investments. He will grow his wealth by investing his savings in the right asset class at the right time. He does this by devoting time to his investments and will have a clear-cut investment strategy. These investors are very few in number; other investors should aspire to be like them.

How to Become a Smart Investor

The smart investor makes money on his investments only for himself. He knows what he wants his investments to do for him. He will take his own investment decisions. He will not get swayed by investment product peddlers. He is able to judge market sentiment accurately, and knows when to buy and sell. You will not find the smart investor holding investments that have no place in his portfolio. In other words, a smart investor will make money for himself by choosing the right investments at the right time. He will use market sentiments to his advantage, and use market information correctly. He will listen to market participants but will not let his decisions get influenced by them. He does not let his ego hinder his investment decisions.

Smart investors have the following traits that one should aspire to emulate:

1. Smart investors stick to investments that they understand, and if that means lack of diversification, so be it. Investors who have belief in the assets they are holding are usually the richest ones.
2. The investment decision is theirs and theirs alone.
3. Smart investors know exactly what they want their investments to do. For example, they do not expect their investment in an insurance linked product to give superior returns.
4. Smart investors invest for returns and not for the sake of saving.
5. Smart investors use to their advantage the very same people who are out to use them. For example, they do business with their stock broker but get him to give them the information they want, and get him to transact the stock they want to buy and sell.
6. Smart investors throw their ego out of the window.

How to Make the Right Investments

Why is it so difficult to select the right investments? The key reason is the large number of investment choices available. Finding the right investment is like finding needles in a haystack. In equity, for example, the choice of investments ranges from the smallest of small-cap stocks to the largest of large-cap stocks. There are over 8,000 stocks listed on the BSE (Bombay Stock Exchange). Investors can also access equity markets through mutual funds that offer products from plain vanilla index funds to capital protected funds. There are portfolio management services (PMS) offered by asset managers and stock brokers. Insurance companies offer investment choices linked to insurance. Investors can diversify geographically by making equity investments across the world, either directly or indirectly through mutual funds. Then there are fixed income investments — from plain vanilla government bonds to exotic derivative products based on different underlying fixed income securities. Fixed income funds are offered by mutual funds as well as PMS providers. Insurance companies link insurance with fixed income. Your pension and provident fund invest exclusively in fixed income investments (This is true in India, but elsewhere they invest in equities too). Then you have other asset classes. Gold, silver, base metals, energy, agri commodities, currencies, and real estate are some of the other asset classes you can find in your investment horizon. How can you make your investments simple and uncomplicated with such a wide range of choices?

Smart investors know what their investments should do for them. In other words, being very clear about what you want your investments to do for you can help you navigate through the vast array of choices available in the investment horizon. If you want high returns, you have your choices; if you want capital protection, you have your choices; if you want steady income, you have your choices. Picking the right investment is made easy once your expectations are clear. You must focus on your investment strategy — and know what to invest in and when to invest. More importantly, you must know what not to invest in; this will help you make money for yourself and not help others make money with your savings.

“Picking the right investment is made easy once your expectations are clear.”

Horses for Courses

This cliché is apt for making right investment choices. It implies that you should select the investment that is suitable for your needs. For instance, if you want high returns, you will never achieve it by investing in capital protected investments, and if you want capital protection, you must stay away from leveraged equity investments. Similarly, if you are a long term investor wishing to save for the future, investing in commodity derivatives or currency futures is not the right choice. If you are willing to risk capital for short term gains, equity futures and options may work for you but if you are unwilling to risk any capital, derivatives are best avoided. Run the horse which is right for the course, and your investments will start working for you.

Direct Investing or Indirect Investing?

There are two routes for making your investments:

1. Invest directly, or
2. Invest through professional money managers.

Direct investments have only one risk — the price of the asset going up or down.

Indirect investments carry many risks, including non-performance by the money manager, intent of fraud by person(s) handling your money, intent to make money from you rather than to make money for you, business continuity of the organization to which you have entrusted your money, legal and compliance misdemeanours by the asset management company managing your money, excessive risk-taking by the fund manager looking after your money, and other such types of risk. The returns from indirect investments, after costs, should be high enough to compensate for the risk and costs incurred. Direct investment, on the other hand, involves the issue of selecting the right investment — whether it is selecting the right stocks, the right bonds, or the right markets. Wrong selection can lead to a high opportunity cost — the cost of not investing elsewhere. You will be the one to have to make this choice; after all you are investing your hard-earned money.

> **“Direct investments have only one risk – the price of the asset going up or down. Indirect investments carry many risks.”**

It is wise to assess each asset class before deciding on whether to opt for direct or indirect investments. Some markets cannot be easily accessed directly; for example, the government bonds market in India. Retail investors face issues of accessing the government bond market due to its institutionalized character where the best price is for a minimum lot of ₹ 5 crore (USD 1.1 million), and small investors are actually encouraged to invest in government bonds through mutual funds. Equity is the most accessible asset class, and information dissemination is high. Other markets, including real estate, gold, silver, currency, and commodities have their own intricacies that need to be assessed in order to decide on whether to invest directly or through the institutional investment route.

Taking the Right Route

Equity

The direct route works best in equities. The market is easily accessible, cost efficient and highly liquid. There is awareness created about equities by the media, including the electronic and print media. If one goes by the media, space given to equities is by far greater than what is given to all other asset classes put together. Equities are also highly scrutinized and regulated as the market performance serves political interests as well. Well-performing equity markets create a "feel good" factor which politicians take advantage of.

Unfortunately, it is also the most abused market. The market is a haven for scamsters and fraudsters who are out to get rich at any cost. Investors constantly fall into their trap and lose capital. Investing in equity markets can be tricky even though the market is the most widely followed and regulated.

Indirect investing in equities may be beneficial if you choose the right products. Plain vanilla products are the best of the lot; the investor is then clear about what he is investing into. For instance, index funds and ETFs (exchange traded funds) help you buy into the equity index and are available at a low cost. Diversified equity funds offer benchmark beating returns but here the investor has to do some research to select the right fund manager. Other products include funds based on market capitalization, such as mid-cap funds and small-cap funds. There are sectoral funds, like information

"The direct route works best in equities. Indirect investing in equities may be beneficial if you choose the right products."

technology funds or consumer goods funds, and there are thematic funds based on themes such as consumption in a geography or energy use in a country. There are funds differentiated on value investing, dividend yields and growth investing. There are country specific funds. The investor has to have the right view on each type of fund before investing in these funds.

Then there are many hybrid funds with equity forming a part of the portfolio. There are capital protected funds that invest in debt and equity in a certain ratio. There are monthly income funds and balanced funds that have a mixture of debt and equity. There are asset allocation funds that have equity as part of their portfolios. The common theme amongst these funds is that if equities perform well the investor will get returns that are higher than fixed income returns, while if equities perform badly, the investor will not lose much capital.

If you want market returns from equities, then hybrids are best avoided.

Fixed Income Investments

Fixed income investments fall into two categories:

1. Pure interest income, and
2. Income from interest plus capital gains.

Pure interest income products include fixed deposits with banks and corporates, pension and provident funds, government and corporate bonds if held to maturity, mutual fund schemes offering interest income, and other government run savings schemes. Income from interest and capital gains comes from investing in government and corporate bonds at a period when interest rates are falling, leading to price gains. You are best advised to invest through mutual funds if you are looking at fixed income returns that include interest income and capital gains.

Here is a golden rule — if you invest in high interest income investments, the risk of default is very high. For example, if a three-year maturity government bond is offering 8 % interest income while a similar maturity corporate bond is offering 13% income, there is a good possibility that the corporate that borrowed the money at 13% may either default in payment of interest and capital, or overrun on its time commitment.

"Here is a golden rule – if you invest in high interest income investments, the risk of default is very high."

Real Estate Investments

Real estate investments are usually done directly by purchasing property. Real estate funds are not very prominent in India though they are popular in markets abroad. Real estate, too, has a concept of dividend yield (rental yield) where the rent received, if the property is let out, yields a certain return on investment. Real estate buyers in India usually look for capital gains but the concept of rental yields is emerging, especially in the commercial real estate space.

Gold and Silver

Gold is a physical investment but with the advent of gold ETFs, gold investments can be held in financial form as well. You can invest in gold ETFs if you hold a view that gold prices will appreciate; otherwise, buying physical gold is better as it gives you comfort of the metal against your skin!

Silver and other jewellery are held mostly in physical form, though globally there are funds that provide access to these metals in the financial form as well. You can invest in these metals, including gold, through the commodity futures market.

Commodities

Commodities, including agricultural commodities and base metals, have a vibrant market and there are many commodity funds operating globally. In India, commodity funds are yet to gain ground due to regulations. Commodity futures markets provide access to these commodities.

Commodities are highly risky and the least understood by individual investors. The market has many variables, including weather, conditions of miners in South America, geo-political instability, and varying government policies. Investors who do not undertake thorough research to understand the commodity market, should not invest in commodities.

Currencies

Currency markets rank very high in trading volumes across the world. The currency futures market has been gaining ground in India too. Investors can invest in USD or euros through the currency futures markets. However, given partial capital controls on the Indian rupee, you can hold only fixed amounts of foreign currency assets, which prevents the market from being an effective investment avenue. Currencies are also prone to large speculation, and the variables that move currency markets are many, including policies followed by other nations and the movements in macro economic variables in regions across the world. If you do not understand currency market fundamentals, it is best to avoid the market.

In summary, for investors with limited knowledge, equity and fixed income are the best choices though the choice itself may depend on many factors as enumerated in the previous chapters. Other asset classes, and investment products based on such asset classes, are best left alone till understood properly.

~

Conclusion

~

How to Make Money Only for Yourself

The world of investments can be confusing. You are constantly bombarded with information. You have a vast array of investment products to choose from. You are solicited by salespersons every hour of the day. Financial planners, with their annuity tables, tell you that you must save a mind-boggling amount to live a decent life after your retirement. You are under pressure to invest and, then, without any thinking or planning, you give in to the pressure. Even the best of us make mistakes under pressure which, in hindsight, look pretty dumb. After having read this book, you can look at investments with a fresh perspective.

> **"Your focus should be to make yourself rich and to keep the bloodhounds at bay."**

Everyone wants a share of your savings, not to make you rich but to make themselves rich. Your focus should be to make yourself rich and to keep the bloodhounds at bay. Even if you have made your money, you will need to re-evaluate your current investments; assess how much of them are benefiting you, and how much are only benefiting others. You need to make your savings work as hard as you did so that you can enjoy the fruits of your labour. All your hard work to build your savings should benefit you. You do not become a successful investor overnight, but you can start the process now.

Now that you have read all the chapters in this book, you will have a fair idea of how to go about your investments. Keep the following points in mind before making any investment and you will soon find that your investments start working for you:

1. Investments must work for you, not for others.
2. You think, therefore you invest.
3. Markets will give different returns at different points of time.
4. There is no certainty of returns from equity markets.
5. You must take your own decisions.
6. You must be conscious of the investment environment.
7. Your investments should work in your lifetime.
8. Assess yourself before you invest.
9. Simple portfolios earn more and cost less to maintain; and
10. Your savings generate the best returns when invested early and liquidated at the right time.

Know Your Limitations

All of us have certain limitations; after all, no one is perfect. When investing, it is important to work within your limitations. Investing is not a marathon, nor is it plain sailing. However, when investments do start working for you, it gives you a great amount of freedom to do a lot more things in your life. The reverse is true if your investments fail you. You get bound to earning a living till retirement, and probably longer. With a profitable investment portfolio, you can live a debt-free life, you can enjoy retirement, and you can spend without feeling guilty. But trying to get an unrealistic return from your investments will work against you. For example, equity investments involve risk capital. If you take on more risk than you can bear, you will find yourself in debt if your investments turn sour. If you have sleepless nights when markets go down, then it's time to reduce your market exposure. Sleeplessness causes disruptions in your daily life, can affect your work, and will end up harming your health. All for some extra returns? It's not worth it!

"With a profitable investment portfolio, you can live a debt-free life, you can enjoy retirement, and you can spend without feeling guilty."

Hand over your portfolio to a professional money manager if you don't have the time or inclination for investing. However, before you do so, take some time to carefully select a suitable one. This effort will benefit you in the long run.

Don't over-extend yourself on property. It's a common mistake investors make, and they suffer as a result. Leveraging for property carries high costs and high risks; be extremely conscious of that. Having to bear more monthly payouts for servicing mortgages than you can afford is very stressful.

Enjoy your profits — and accept your losses with equanimity. If you are able to do that, you have worked within your limitations and have made the right investment decisions.

~

Glossary

Asset Management Company (AMC): The firm that manages the mutual fund schemes.

Analyst: Person who does research.

Arbitrage Funds: Mutual funds schemes that generate returns by playing on price differentials, especially between the cash market and the derivative market.

Asian Market Bubble: The collapse of the "tiger economies" such as Thailand, Malaysia, Korea, and Indonesia in the late 1990s due to excessive external debt.

Asset Allocation: Portfolios that are invested in different types of asset classes, e.g. bonds, equities, property, commodity, etc.

Asset Class: A group of securities with similar overlap characteristics.

Bear Market: A phase of the market when asset prices are going down.

Benchmark: The main index used for reference.

Benchmark Bonds: Regularly traded bonds that are used to construct yield curves.

Bond Trader: Person who buys and sells government and corporate bonds with the intention of making profits.

Bond Yields: The rate of return on bonds. Bond yields are inversely related to price.

Broad Market: The benchmark index.

BSE IT: BSE Information Technology Index.

BSE CG: BSE Capital Goods Index.

BSE Sensex: An index comprising 30 stocks listed on the Bombay Stock Exchange (BSE).

Bull Market: Period of the market when asset prices are going up.

Compounded Annual Growth Rate (CAGR): Compounded Annual Growth Rate is calculated by the formula p(1+r/100)^n, where p is principal, r is the return and n is the time period.

Chief Financial Officer (CFO): Executive responsible for the finance and treasury functions of a firm.

Cash Market: Market where the buyer has to make full payment for purchasing of an asset or deliver the asset against a sale.

Contract: An agreement between two counterparties.

Concentrated Portfolios: Portfolios that have few stocks with each stock forming a large chunk of the portfolio.

Corporate Treasurer: Person who heads the treasury.

Cross Currency Swap: Derivative based on two different currencies.

Credit Risk: Risk of default on debt by a borrower.

Credit Rating Agencies: Entities that rate the capability of debt issuers to repay debt and service interest payments.

Credit Crisis of 2008: The crisis occurred when banks were taking heavy leveraged positions on mortgage loans that were given to sub-prime (close to default) borrowers. The banks suffered huge losses due to loan defaults as property prices crashed leading to crashing equity prices across the world.

CRISIL Rating: CRISIL is an Indian rating agency that rates corporate bonds, IPOs, etc. to reflect the risk to principal.

Currency Derivatives: Derivatives based on currency pairs such as USD/INR, USD/JPY, EURO/USD, etc.

Debt Syndication: One or many lenders to a borrower usually arranged by a syndicator.

Depressions: A phase when asset prices are down and sentiments are low in the market.

Derivative: A financial instrument that derives its value from an underlying asset such as equities, bond, commodities or currencies.

Derivative Market: Market where derivatives are traded.

Dow Jones Industrial Average (DJIA): Dow Jones Industrial Average is an index of 30 stocks traded on the New York Stock Exchange.

Equated Monthly Instalments (EMI): Equated Monthly Instalments paid by the borrower to the lender for servicing interest and principal repayments on loans.

Entrepreneur: Person who commences a new business.

External Debt: Debt that is denominated in currencies other than the currency of residence.

Expiry: Maturity of a contract.

Exotic Derivatives: Derivative products that are highly complicated in nature.

First Generation Entrepreneur: First time entrepreneur.

Fixed Income: Investments in instruments other than equity instruments that generate steady fixed cash flows.

Floor Trader: Person who buys and sells securities on the floor of the exchange following an open outcry system where orders are shouted. In this electronic trading age, floor trading has been completely replaced by electronic trading in many countries including India.

Forward Currency Contract: Entails the buyer to either sell or buy currencies at a forward date at a pre-decided fixed price.

Futures: Contract to buy or sell an asset at a future date.

Fund Manager: Professional money manager.

Fund Rating Agencies: Entities that rate and rank schemes floated by product manufacturers.

Guaranteed Return Products: Products where capital and return are guaranteed.

Hang Seng Index: Stock index comprising of 45 stocks listed in the Hong Kong Stock Exchange.

Hedge: An offsetting transaction to protect portfolio value.

Hedge Fund Manager: Loosely regulated fund managers.

Hybrids: Fund schemes that have a mixture of different asset classes.

Insurance Premium: Premium paid on insurance policy.

Initial Public Offering (IPO): Initial Public Offering of equities or bonds in the form of public issue.

Illiquidity: Not easily saleable.

Investment Philosophy: The basic premise on which a fund manager makes his investments.

Investment Quack: A so-called expert on markets and investment.

Investment Banker: Person who advises companies for a fee.

Jakarta Composite Index: Index of all stocks that trade on the Indonesia Stock Exchange.

Large, Mid and Small Cap Stocks: Stocks based on their market capitalization.

Leverage: Ratio of borrowing to equity.

Liquidity: Cash in the system.

Leveraged Funds: Funds that use leverage to generate returns.

Market Bubble: Bubbles occur when asset prices reach unsustainable heights.

Market Correction: Temporary fall in prices.

Market Capitalization: Number of shares outstanding × price. Market capitalization is usually on free float, that is, the outstanding number of shares is calculated after taking out the promoters' holding.

Market Valuation: Ratios such as price earnings ratio, price to book value ratio, etc.

Mark to Market: Profit and loss of holding a security due to change in market values.

Margin: Initial amount paid for entering into a derivative contract.

Multibagger: A stock that has seen its price go up by several times.

Nasdaq Composite: Index of stocks traded on the Nasdaq Stock Exchange.

Net Asset Value (NAV): Net Asset Value is the unit value of a mutual fund scheme.

New Fund Offer: Fresh schemes launched by mutual funds.

Nifty Index: The Nifty index or the S&P CNX Nifty is a fifty stock index listed on the National Stock Exchange of India (NSE).

Nifty Index Fund: A mutual fund scheme that mirrors the Nifty index.

Options: Right to buy or sell an asset at a certain price.

Out-perform: An investment that gives better returns than a comparable investment.

Over-subscription: Demand for shares on offer is higher than the number of shares on offer.

Portfolio Management Scheme (PMS): Portfolio Management Scheme providers manage portfolios of individual investors on a fee-based or a profit-sharing basis. They are different from mutual funds in the sense that they are not collective schemes and there are no units allotted against investments.

Portfolio: Investments of an investor.

Private Equity: Equity investments in companies that have not floated IPOs.

Proprietary Trader: Person who buys and sells stocks, bonds, commodities, etc. with his own money with the intention of making profits.

Program Trading: Computers are programmed to trade.

Provident Funds and Pension Funds: Saving schemes for the public.

Promoter: Majority owner or management control of a company.

Product Manufacturer: Financial services firm that floats investment schemes charging management fees for the same.

Product Distributor: Person who sells for commission, financial products manufactured by a financial services firm.

Qualified Institutional Placement (QIP): Qualified Institutional Placement is a private placement of equity to institutional investors.

Research: In-depth analysis.

Relative Trading: Trading based on movements of one security with another.

Risk Profile: Risk taking ability.

Risk: Potential loss of capital.

Rolling Over: Carrying forward a contract to the next month of expiry.

Russia Debt Crisis: Russia defaulted on its debt in the late 1990s leading to many lenders facing losses.

Systematic Investment Plans (SIP): Systematic Investment Plans make investors invest periodically into mutual fund schemes.

Second Generation Entrepreneur: Person who takes over existing businesses.

Secular: One way

Securities: Stocks and bonds.

Sector Funds: Mutual fund schemes that invest in specific stock sectors, e.g. Technology sector fund.

Shareholders' Wealth: The wealth effect from ownership of a company's stocks.

Sovereign Funds: Government money that is managed by government run asset management company.

Stock Broker: Person who buys and sells securities on the stock exchange.

Straddling the Index: Buying stocks based on their weight in the index.

Structured Products: Products that are manufactured to adhere to a certain risk return profile.

Technical Analyst: Person who predicts future prices using past data.

Telecom Spectrum: Telecom companies require bandwidth for providing 2G and 3G communication services and the government licenses out this bandwidth.

Term Insurance: Insurance cover that entails payment of a single or series of premiums in return for benefits.

Thematic Funds: Mutual fund schemes that invest in specific themes, e.g. consumer driven stocks.

Treasury: The department that handles all the money of the firm.

Under-perform: An investment that gives lower returns than a comparable investment.

Unit linked Policies: Insurance products that bundles investment and risk cover.

Yield Curves: Chart of yields across varying bond maturities of similar credit quality.

Valuation: Value of an asset in terms of market price to company's earnings or in terms of future cash flows.

Where are the Customers Yachts: Author Fred Schwed.